Connect!

Connect!

Tim Jeffery with Steve Chalke

*To the countless people from many cultures
around the world who have enriched
our lives and helped us to learn
to love God's 'divine mosaic'.*

Contents

Preface   ix
Foreword   xi
Acknowledgements   xiii

1   Globalisation: The Way the World Works   1
2   Postmodernity: A New Pair of Glasses   23
3   The Global Church – All Change!   37
4   Trend-spotting   51
5   Musical Chairs   63
6   Becoming a Global Family   85
7   The Connect! Covenant   96
8   Spice it up!   104
9   Where do we Start?   131
10 Doing it Well   146

A Final Word   159

Preface

God is doing something new and radical in our time. It is our belief that we are at the beginning of a radical shift in global mission. For two hundred years, through many alterations and enhancements, the Christian community in the west has built up a shared understanding of world mission. The evidence seems to be growing however that the 'traditional' ways of doing and conceiving of mission are no longer working as once they did. Mission agencies are seeing changes but many are unsure about what to make of them or what the future might hold. A number of respected mission thinkers are talking about change.

In writing this book we are seeking to encourage a revolution that is actually already underway. We are trying to point out the tidal wave that is building out at sea. It's not yet very visible but as it approaches it will grow until it sweeps away our current understanding of global mission and replaces it with something very different. Our desire is to play a part in helping the church in the UK and beyond to surf this wave rather than be washed away by it.

Connect! is not a book: we hope that it will be the beginning of a movement. A movement that takes hold of the amazing opportunities before us, helping the church to act like the greatest global network the world has ever known in order to bring the Good News of God's love to every corner of the planet.

Foreword

Because of the emergence of rapid and relatively inexpensive forms of transportation, Christians have, as of late, become directly involved with people in Third World countries. Far off mission fields are now part of a global village, and huge numbers of western Christians now visit and work with churches in the poor countries of the world. They want to encourage indigenous churches and help them address the problems associated with the poverty faced daily by Third World peoples.

The commitments and generosity of the rich Christians of western countries that flow from these involvements have resulted in much good, but too often that good has had painful side effects. There have been many instances in which western Christians, upon seeing the poverty of the poor churches of the southern hemisphere, have given money in ways that create the kind of dependency that disempowers the very people they want to help. Sometimes the work groups that have built schools, clinics and other buildings, have taken desperately needed jobs away from indigenous people. I know of one case in which a church group from the United States built and staffed a state-of-the-art clinic in Haiti, not realizing that they were competing with a struggling nearby clinic that had been established by some dedicated Haitian Christian doctors. The clinic was eventually forced to close. This short, but very important book, explains how, through the use of modern technology, such pitfalls can be avoided.

Ray Kurzweil, in his groundbreaking book, *The Age of Spiritual Machines*, made it clear that computers have changed the future of the human race. *Connect!* gives us some idea of how the ways in which Christians do missionary work should be changed because of the accessibility of computers. The authors introduce us to the Connect! Covenant, which is a whole new way for people around the world to use the Internet to help each other to carry out the Great Commission. Connect! Covenant enables Christians from different countries to learn from each other's experiences what to do and what not to do as they endeavor to minister cross-culturally. That makes this book a 'must read' for those who have missions on their minds.

Tony Campolo
Eastern University
St. Davids, PA
USA

Acknowledgements

Many people have provided inspiration for this book and had a hand in shaping its contents. First and foremost we want to acknowledge Ros Johnson for the year of her life that she gave to Oasis and the development of *Connect!* She has been an invaluable help in undertaking the research behind this book and working on examples and text. It would not have made it into print without her.

Thanks to Richard Tiplady for his support, advice and input to the content of *Connect!* and the other mission thinkers and practitioners that have contributed to our thinking.

We are most grateful also to the many church leaders and members who gave generously of their time to tell us what their churches are doing in global mission. Their stories not only illustrate but also helped to shape this book, and we hope they will prove an inspiration to others.

Special thanks to the team at Oasis and particularly within Oasis Global Action both in the UK and around the world, who have had such an impact in inspiring the content of this book and been so patient during its construction.

1

Globalisation:
The Way the World Works

What is globalisation?

The people of the world are becoming more and more interconnected and interdependent, whether they like it or not. This process can be summed up in the term globalisation, and it affects just about every area of our lives. We can trace its origins to Christopher Columbus, the Vikings, the Roman Empire, or even further back, but it was really in the twentieth century that we saw the process beginning to take massive strides. And it was not until the 1990s that we recognised globalisation as the dominant force for change.

> DEFINITIONS
>
> **Globalisation** is the process that is making us more *interconnected* and *interdependent*.
>
> *Interconnected* –
> being more joined together
>
> *Interdependent* –
> being more reliant on each other

Some milestones in the relentless development of globalisation

- 1800s – Europe spreads its influence to the farthest parts of the globe by carving up much of the world into colonies.
- 1940s – Some major global institutions are created – the United Nations, World Bank and International Monetary Fund.
- 1989 – The end of the Cold War signals the success of free market capitalism as the dominant world order.
- 1990s – the Internet begins to take off as the new global highway for communication, trade, information and economic development.

Consider for a moment the changes experienced by someone like the Queen Mother whose life began at the beginning of the 1900s and ended shortly after the close of the twentieth century.

- Communication became instant in the transition from post to phone, fax and email.
- Roads, railways, and air travel have reduced international journey times from weeks and months to a matter of hours: we can now go for a fortnight's holiday to Peru, New Zealand or the Arctic.
- Produce that was seasonal is now available the year round: beans and flowers from Kenya, apples from Chile, avocados from Israel ... the sources are many and far-flung.
- News of events from the far corners of the earth that once might have taken weeks to reach us, can now be watched live on TV coming via satellites that encircle the earth.

● In London there are restaurants offering the national food of Lebanon, Thailand, Nepal, Ethiopia, Japan ... the list goes on and on.

Does globalisation = Americanisation?

To answer this question it may help to visualise globalisation as a vast motorway built largely by western countries, circling the globe and bearing all sorts of traffic. There are feeder roads to each country, and in principle one country and its people have as much right as anyone else to send traffic onto the highway. However most of the traffic currently comes from North America and western Europe, though some vehicles may have parts made in several countries.

Incoming traffic inevitably has an effect at its destinations. Not only is there an environmental impact from the volume of traffic, but also the goods the vehicles deliver can deeply affect the economy, customs and outlook of those on the receiving end. Some of this impact can be beneficial. Local people may improve their standard of living and the way they relate to each other. There is also an opportunity to export their own products to new and distant markets. But many countries lack the motivation, wealth, opportunity, vehicles or goods to send traffic on the global highway. So for most countries the inward carriageway is far wider and busier than the outward carriageway, and for many the outward carriageway is virtually non-existent.

In this analogy the infrastructure of globalisation (in the form of advances in transport, technology, communications, trade, the media) owes much to what was done by western countries in the nineteenth and twentieth centuries, with the United States increasingly dominant. And at present much of what is 'exported' around the world with the aid of globalisation is American – whether in trade, economics, political and social ideas, or culture. But it is possible for other countries and cultures to use the same globalised infrastructure to export their own commercial, ideological or cultural products: witness the recent impact of Bollywood in Britain and North America. In the future the flow of 'goods' along the globalisation motorway could see far more goods in transit, from many more varied sources, than is evident now.

Globalisation – how it affects us

Globalisation as a process or force in our world is hard to get a handle on or define. It's a bit like the wind – we can't see it and pin it down, but we do see very clearly its effects in the world around us. Similarly, we can point to many manifestations of globalisation in just about every area of human activity. Such manifestations in the field of communications, technology or banking are things that we can recognise as changing and having a growing impact on our lives.

Let's have a closer look at some of these areas that globalisation is affecting and try to understand how this impacts our lives.

Globalisation and the new global economy

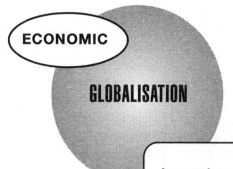

ECONOMIC

GLOBALISATION

It is in the realm of economics that globalisation is having its most obvious and controversial impact. There are those that see the development of a single global economy as being the greatest hope for the future wealth of humankind. There are others

> **Average income** in the world's 20 richest countries is 37 times larger than the average income in the 20 poorest countries.
>
> Over 1.2 billion people in the world live on less than $1 a day.

who argue that it is the greatest evil, widening the gap between rich and poor and giving even greater power to the rich nations and massive global corporations. The World Trade Organisation is gaining power in trying to build a global trading system but there are those organising massive rallies to protest against what they see as exploitative global trading systems – it's a confusing picture.

Economic globalisation is basically about the development of a dominant global economic system built on a free market, capitalist ideology. The amount of money flowing around the world every day in investment and foreign exchange markets is thought to be between one and two trillion US dollars. The economies of the world are becoming increasingly linked and interdependent so that what happens on one side of the world can have significant implications for a national economy somewhere else.

So what are the driving forces behind this global economy?

Capitalism has unquestionably emerged as the dominant economic ideology in our world. Currency speculator George Soros equates globalisation with market fundamentalism – like religious fundamentalism but with the free market as its God. Behind this ideology lies the desire to generate wealth and to maximise economic efficiency – from one perspective both laudable and understandable aims. Turning the prism a little, however,

> The sudden collapse of the Thai economy in 1997 sent shock waves around the other economies of the Far East and triggered a flight of capital from the region. A downturn in world commodity prices followed and ultimately, like a row of collapsing dominoes, almost no national economy in the world was left unaffected by what proved to be the first truly global financial crisis of the new era of globalisation.

it is easy to see how materialism, consumerism and simple human greed are given free rein within this system.

The result in some countries has been extraordinary economic growth and greater wealth creation, from which many have benefited. It has helped to create a consumers' paradise for those who can afford it, with shopping malls around the world offering an infinite variety of goods of all kinds, and ever more sophisticated means of customising products to suit the individual. Infrastructure has been developed, education has become more widely available – there are lots of very positive results of this economic development – for some.

> **THE GLOBAL ECONOMY – A CONSUMER'S PARADISE**
>
> Some clothing chains have begun to offer garments made to measure. Once customers have chosen a style, they are invited to go into a booth for their measurements to be taken by laser and then wired to a factory for making up. The completed garment will be delivered to the customer two or three weeks later.

The freeing up of world trade through the spread of free market values and the breaking down of trade barriers is supposed to bring greater wealth for all. Yet many less-developed countries have suffered, and corruption in some of these countries has often made a bad situation worse. So while we see an overall rise in wealth worldwide, there is a widening gap between rich and poor nations with some seeming to be totally left out. The divide is not simply between nations – it is often the shocking contrast of wealth and poverty within one nation that brings home the reality of some benefiting and others falling further behind. The plight of the children living and working on city streets (estimated at around

In 2002 rice produced by subsidised American farmers was dumped on the local market in Ghana, throwing local rice producers out of business. As well as seriously damaging this sector of the Ghanaian economy it cast previously productive members of society into poverty and unemployment in a country where few alternative occupations are available.

150 million worldwide) gives tragic evidence that those least able to fend for themselves are the ones who often suffer most.

The global picture is pretty gruesome and as God's people seeking justice for all peoples of the world – we have work to do. Trade barriers create anything but a level playing field for the poorest, keeping power and wealth in the hands of the rich. Massive Transnational Corporations (TNCs) have incomes the size of large countries and are able to operate largely outside national frameworks of regulation and control. The rich get richer, the poor get poorer – is this the kind of world that we as the people of God are happy to be part of and benefit from?

There is much about economic globalisation that is undoubtedly wrong, exploitative and against the values of the kingdom of God. Many people equate globalisation with these economic realities, thus leading to the anti-globalisation movement and a very negative attitude towards anything with the 'G' label. This is an unfortunate connection. Globalisation is about much more than money.

Globalisation and technology, communications and transport

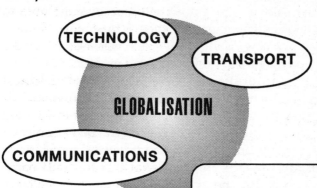

The growth of communication has been a significant factor in enabling the spread of globalisation into every

> The total number of phone calls made across the world in 1984 is now made in one day.

other area of human activity. There has been massive development of the global telecommunications infrastructure with some poorer countries leapfrogging the traditional system of wires and poles and going straight to a majority mobile network. Communication satellites now encircle the earth making it possible to use a satellite phone anywhere on the planet. We are becoming used to an environment in which we can always be reached and in which we need never be out of touch. The speed, efficiency and coverage of global communications is also a key factor in underpinning the new global economy.

Developments in technology have been equally stunning. Prime amongst these has to be the development of computers. The speed of computers to process information doubles about every 18 months. To give some idea of the impact of this, compare the development of computers since the 1960s to the humble automobile. If cars had increased in speed at the same rate as computers, the average family saloon would now be doing over 1.5 million mph! Or look at it another way: there is now more computing power in a new 7 series BMW than was used to put the first man on the moon! Computers and microchips are now an integral part of life and have been the technological backbone of much of the development of globalisation.

Although our cars may not be going much faster than forty years ago, the number of cars on the planet is growing exponentially and the rise of air travel has transformed our attitude towards international travel – and some would say, made the world a smaller place. These advances have, for example, made possible the growth of mass tourism, which has enabled many people to discover for themselves new places and different cultures.

Globalisation and knowledge and information

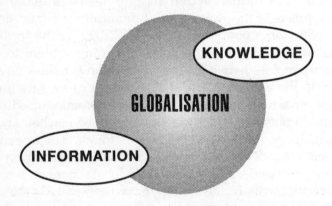

The development of computers, telecommunications and the Internet has seen a fantastic spread in access to knowledge and information of all kinds. Whilst many of us may at times struggle to find what we want on the Net, the volume of information that can be accessed is truly awesome and growing every day. Students from poor communities who may have access to very meagre information through a handful of textbooks, can now access a wealth of information from across the world.

'The days when governments could isolate their people from understanding what life was like beyond their borders or even beyond their village are over. Life outside can't be trashed and made to look worse than it is. And life inside can't be propagandized and made to look better than it is … We all increasingly know how each other lives – no matter how isolated you may think a country might be'[1]

Globalisation and society and culture

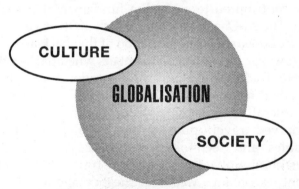

The constant change and fast pace of life that are part of living in a globalised world make many around the world

[1] Thomas Friedman, *The Lexus and the Olive Tree* (London: HarperCollins, 2000), p.67.

feel uneasy and insecure. Even our governments often have little power to resist the forces that are driving us on relentlessly to a future that we have not chosen and may fear and dislike. In many countries such reactions have resulted in a resurgence of interest in local identity and customs, including in some a growth in religious fundamentalism and hostility to all things western. Sadly, in countries in the Middle East and Asia there is a tendency to see Christianity as a western import, and persecution of local Christians has often been stepped up.

The attack on the World Trade Center in New York on 11 September 2001 provides a graphic illustration of the stresses globalisation can impose. The Center had become a symbol of the dominant economic force of free market capitalism and of American/western economic, political and cultural power. These intertwined factors are perceived by many Muslims to pose a threat to their traditional society and values, and contributed to a Muslim fundamentalist backlash. The Al-Qaeda and their attack on the twin towers are an extreme manifestation of that backlash.

However the Al-Qaeda members who attacked the World Trade Center and the Pentagon themselves benefited from many developments that are part of the overall globalising process. Because of greatly improved travel opportunities, freer movement of peoples and technological progress, the young Muslims involved were able to travel in western countries, obtain a western education and learn how to fly aircraft. Telephone, satellite and internet systems enabled them to keep in touch with each other and receive instructions across continents. When the attack on the Center and on the Pentagon in Washington occurred, similar technological advances enabled millions around the world to watch the horrific events unfolding live on their television screens.

McDonald's, Coca Cola and Nike are all examples of global brands that few corners of the world are untouched by. In many ways it feels like a global culture is developing – particularly amongst the young. The 2002 Football World Cup showed vividly how fast and strongly fashions and enthusiasms now cross national boundaries. We watch the same matches, see the same news on CNN, listen to the same music on MTV, wear the same clothes, surf the same Internet sites etc. To many, this developing global culture looks suspiciously American, provoking strong reactions by many to the perceived global dominance of the US.

At the same time as we are seeing the development of this global culture, there is an opposite reaction occurring. As well as globalisation we are seeing localisation and fragmentation taking place. In the sea of sameness across the world, people are seeking some identity and distinguishing factor (remember the dramatic surfacing of ethnic divisions in the Balkans). Indeed

During the 2002 Football World Cup Japan defeated its old enemy Russia. Disappointed and enraged football fans in Moscow went on a rampage which left a trail of destruction, two people dead and 50 people in hospital.

According to a report in The Times of 11 June, the Russian brand of hooliganism was modelled, explicitly and self-consciously, on the British version. Unofficial fan clubs took British names, adopted British slogans, watched videos about British football hooligans, and revered the British football thug.

it appears that ethnic identity is becoming more, rather than less, important. At the same time as the EU is growing in scope and influence, we are seeing the development of Regional Assemblies across the UK. Globalisation and localisation are opposite forces and yet the intensity of each is growing.

Globalisation, politics, warfare and terrorism

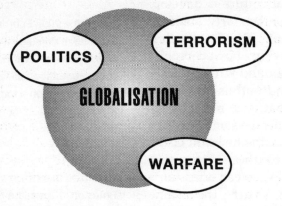

On the political scene there has been a growing awareness of the extent to which we are all interconnected, and how much events in one corner of the globe can lead to repercussions in the opposite corner. The many international organisations and agreements that now exist show that the need is recognised for a framework in which nations can get together to discuss the problems that arise in an interconnected world and try to resolve them. At present though, they seem woefully inadequate for tackling some of the more difficult issues that have been thrown up by the world's growing interconnectedness. They also present real dilemmas for some nations for whom some form of sacrifice may appear to be the price of such agreements. The Kyoto agreement on environmental pollution is a great example of nations working together and yet it was rejected by the US – the greatest polluter of them all – on grounds of economic self-interest. In a globalised world, we desperately need ways of working together for the good of the human race as a whole. We have work to do …

Globalisation has made it possible for the major developed countries to conduct wars halfway around the world, as the war in Afghanistan confirmed in 2001. It also means that weapons produced in developed countries may be bought and used to devastating effect in the pursuit of tribal conflicts in countries such as Sierra Leone.

Globalisation has also given ruthless individuals and groups from right outside the traditional structures of political or military power new ways to make their presence felt. The cultural and religious tensions which globalisation has helped to create, allied with the free movement of peoples and the widespread availability of technical know-how, which are also products of globalisation, all combine to make it possible for attacks to be launched against perceived enemies by a variety of horrific means. National boundaries have little effect in containing threats of this kind. Biological, chemical or explosive attacks are now a chilling possibility in almost any corner of the globe, as the Bali bomb in 2002 demonstrated.

Globalisation and ideas and beliefs

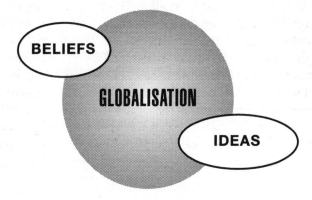

In the realm of ideas and beliefs, globalisation makes it much easier for every religion or belief structure to become global in scope. The spread of Christianity to every continent of the world

> 20 per cent of American born-again Christians believe in reincarnation and 26 per cent in astrology, according to a Gallup poll (quoted in *Christianity Today*, 7 August 2000).

was greatly helped by the improved communications and transport of the last two hundred years or so. The same improvements (easier travel, the media, etc.), along with global migration, have meant that people in 'Christian' nations have become much more aware of other religions such as Hinduism and Islam, if only because followers of other faiths now often live down the street. In the minds of many this has undermined the validity of Christianity's claims to be the only way to God, and believing Christians themselves have not been immune from the resulting uncertainty nor from contagion by beliefs which sit uneasily with orthodox Christianity.

The penetration of western liberal ideals of equality and human rights into other cultures has also helped improve the lot of women and children in many countries, ensuring for them greater economic and social opportunities.

Despotic regimes that repress and abuse their own citizens can also be held to account at the bar of world opinion and suffer in consequence. This revolution in communication and information also means that people can be mobilised in various ways to take up the cause of people halfway round the globe.

> In the 1990s Burma was a repressive regime which had been isolated on the international stage. This had not deterred a number of multinationals such as

Philips, Motorola and Carlsberg from setting up business there, attracted by the favourable operating conditions on offer. They had not reckoned however on the activists and consumers in western countries who targeted them through the Free Burma Campaign and, by threatening a consumer boycott of their products, persuaded them to pull out.

Globalisation and the environment

20 per cent of the world's population produce 80 per cent of the greenhouse gasses which contribute to global warming.

The environmental cost of the rush for economic growth and material improvement is also often borne by those who have not been responsible for producing the pollutants that damage their environment, destroy livelihoods, reduce wildlife habitats and contribute to global warming. The biggest polluters of the planet are the ones who can afford to make changes, but are so often not willing to agree to any move that might affect their standard of living –

whatever the long term environmental impact. Our growing understanding of the way the world's ecosystem and environment works is helping us to quantify our impact on our planet and realise just how interconnected we are as a human race sharing one home together.

In the coming years, our shared environment, in particular its finite ability to cope with human activity, looks set to become a growing issue. Water for instance is becoming an increasingly rare commodity for millions of people and it is predicted that the wars and conflicts of the future are as likely to be over access to water as over political or ethnic differences. It may be possible to bring fresh fruit half way round the world, but what is the environmental cost of doing this? If this cost were somehow added to the price on the shelf, would it in fact make a fundamental difference to world trade? As the world continues full tilt down the road of globalisation we have got to face up to these hard realities.

Is globalisation evil?

When the zip fly was first introduced to the world, Christians vehemently opposed it as a work of the devil that would lead people astray. Cinema was similarly opposed, as was the Internet more recently. Too often our tendency is to demonise new things that we don't understand in our fear that they may be used for evil purposes.

Many people equate globalisation with the development of the global economy. It is easy to paint a picture of economic globalisation that shows how destructive it is for the poor, how it concentrates power in the hands of the wealthy, how it is ruining the very planet on which we depend for our survival, and leads us to sign up to the anti-globalisation lobby. The emerging global economic order is not however the last or defining word on globalisation. As the process of growing interconnectedness and interdependence, globalisation manifests itself in every area of human activity – one of which is economic. It is human beings who take the tools, technologies and possibilities offered by globalisation and decide to turn them to good ends or bad, to the advantage of a privileged minority or the good of the poor and excluded. Globalisation needs to undergo a 'humanising' process, to take account of its impact on human beings and the environment. Wouldn't it be great if Christians were to take a lead in this? The Jubilee Campaign, which persuaded many governments and financial institutions to cancel the debts of the poorest nations in 2000, has shown what can be done.

When the Industrial Revolution hit Great Britain in the late eighteenth and nineteenth centuries, conditions in the factories and mines were appalling. Both adults and children worked long hours in dreadful conditions for minimal reward. But concerned campaigners roused the conscience of the nation, and legislation was introduced to ensure that working conditions were made progressively more humane. One of the leading campaigners was a Christian, Lord Shaftesbury, who had a huge influence on improving conditions for the industrial poor. Thus, over time, the Industrial Revolution was humanised, helping its benefits to become more widely spread.

Globalisation is not, of itself, evil or bad. What people decide to do with the opportunities it presents, can be. To be anti-globalisation is to try to turn back the tide and to miss the amazing opportunities it presents to us for the development of God's kingdom. There are undoubtedly things that people have done with the process of globalisation that reflect our fallen, selfish nature, but there are also plenty of examples of how people have engaged with it to use the opportunities it presents for good ends.

A global church with a global mission

There are Christians in every nation, and almost a third of the human race consider themselves to belong to the Christian faith. In fact, the church is the greatest global network that has ever existed – we may never have seen ourselves in this light, but it is true. Until now we have not thought globally but for the first time in human history, the mindset, technology and infrastructure that are part of globalisation present us with the opportunity to become the global family that we are destined to be. In a globalised, interconnected world we have the tools we need to truly be God's global community – a global church.

We *could* choose to use globalisation to create the world's biggest club for the benefit and enjoyment of its members. Whilst there is great value in having a global identity for the church, we don't believe that this is the end to which we should put the opportunities before us. The reason for recognising the global nature of the church has to be the fantastic opportunity it presents us to work together at a global mission. This is our destiny for the twenty-first century:

> *To be global Christians, part of a global church*
> *working together on God's global mission.*

Summary

❏ The world is becoming increasingly interconnected and interdependent – we call this process globalisation.

❏ Globalisation is now the dominant force in shaping human development and affects cultures, economies, communication, technology, politics – in fact just about everything!

❏ Globalisation is not in itself evil (some of the ways we have chosen to use it are) but should be seen as morally neutral.

❏ The church is the greatest global network – it just doesn't realise it or act like it yet.

❏ Globalisation provides the church with a massive opportunity to become an effective global family, working together in God's global mission.

We may be excited or appalled by globalisation. But if we have some understanding of what is happening – not just in our own country but around the world – we can begin to grapple with the challenges posed and seize the opportunities offered. Read on ...

Questions for discussion

1. In what ways do you personally and your community appear to benefit from globalisation?

2. In what ways do you think you are worse off because of globalisation?

3. What do you think the Christian's attitude should be to the whole phenomenon of globalisation?

4. What does it mean to you and your church community to be part of a global church? In what ways (if any) do you see evidence of this fact in your church life?

Further resources on globalisation

Thomas Friedman, *The Lexus and the Olive Tree* (London: HarperCollins, 2000) – a vivid, readable account of globalisation and what it means for people around the world.

Charles Reed (ed.), *Development Matters: Christian Perspectives on Globalisation* (London: Church House Publishing, 2001) – a thoughtful survey of aspects of globalisation from a Christian standpoint.

Tom Sine, *Mustard Seed versus McWorld* (London: Monarch, 1999) – highlights the growing disparity in wealth between countries of the northern and southern hemispheres as globalisation advances. Sine challenges Christians to adopt radically different values and agendas from those of secular western society.

Naomi Klein, *No Logo* (London: Flamingo, 2001) – a dense but readable and well-researched account of how the branding of our society by designer labels is often at the expense of exploited workers in the Two-Thirds World.

2

Postmodernity:
A New Pair of Glasses

Each of us has our own way of looking at life and the world around us, and trying to make sense of them. Our outlook is founded on some basic assumptions or mental models about the world and the way it works. These assumptions usually develop subconsciously, so many of us may not even know that we have them. But they have a powerful influence on the way we behave and think.

Some of our assumptions will be personal and based mainly on our character, upbringing and experience, such as the belief that I am (or am not) loveable. But other assumptions are shared because they are drawn from the underlying worldview of the society in which we live. The underlying worldview, values and norms of behaviour of a culture are collectively called a 'paradigm'.

Post what?

It is now widely accepted that western society is undergoing a fundamental shift in its basic paradigm. Paradigm shifts usually happen only once every few hundred years – so there are some very profound changes going on at present without many of us even being aware that they are happening! Paradigm shifts seem to happen when a combination of events and new philosophical thinking on the way life is (often the result of reflecting on events) leads to the population at large gradually accepting new interpretations of reality and new values. It takes decades before a new worldview (paradigm) is fully absorbed into most people's thinking, but it will make its presence felt long before that. What we are now seeing is a shift from 'modernity' to 'postmodernity'.

Definitions

Paradigm shift – a fundamental change in the underlying assumptions of a whole culture.

Modernity – the collection of beliefs and attitudes that dominated western culture from around the mid-eighteenth century to the late twentieth century; characterised by the view that humanity can make steady progress towards a state of freedom, material prosperity and happiness by the application of reason and the use of science and technology.

Postmodernity – the outlook and attitudes that began to dominate western culture in the last quarter of the twentieth century. Postmodernity rejects the basic assumptions of modernity especially the beliefs in universal truth and general progress, and is characterised by an openness to a variety of different options and ways of thinking.

The main assumptions of modernity were crystallised in the eighteenth century 'Enlightenment' period and centred on:

● Belief in the power of the human mind to discover ultimate truth;

- Belief that humanity was embarked on a course of steady progress towards general prosperity and happiness, through the application of science, technology and economic development; and

- Belief that the world and all human activity could and should be controlled to eliminate uncertainty and risk.

This confident outlook suited the expansion of western Europe and North America in the nineteenth century and the rapid industrial and technological progress made in that period. However events of the twentieth century such as two world wars, the Holocaust and the nuclear bomb, cast serious doubt on its optimistic premises. The shift to 'postmodernity' that started in the last few decades of the twentieth century (and is still going on) is essentially a reaction to, and rejection of, many of the basic assumptions of 'modernity'.

> 'If recent history can be likened to a sea voyage, postmodernity represents mutiny – the determination to wrest the steering mechanism from the self-appointed owners of the ship.'[1]

This means that in some ways postmodernity is easier to describe by what it rejects than by what it affirms. For a start, it is very suspicious of the idea of any absolute truth or universally true 'story', whether that story be about the inevitable march of progress or the claim that Jesus Christ is the only way to God.

---

[1] J. Andrew Kirk, 'Following Modernity and Postmodernity', *Mission Studies*, vol. XVI (2000), pp.1111-12.

Comparison of some key differences between modernity and postmodernity

Modernity	Postmodernity
• Absolute truth can be grasped by human reasoning.	• Loss of faith in absolutes. What matters is what is true for you.
• Reason is the ultimate means by which truth can be discovered, nature explored, and progress made.	• Reason is not supreme. Experience, spirituality and intuition are equally important.
• The independent, 'heroic' individual is capable of transforming the world.	• Still individualistic but loss of self-confidence – multiple alternative identities are on offer. Image and style more important than substance.
• Confidence, optimism, idealism.	• Cynicism, humour and parody, lack of a sense of meaning and purpose.
• Steady progress is being made by humanity towards greater happiness and prosperity for everyone.	• The idea of progress is at best doubtful, at worst an illusion.
• One overarching world story – the march of progress.	• Many stories – none universally true.
• Emphasis on orthodoxy and conformity to norms in society.	• Importance of diversity and listening to minority voices. Pluralism.

• Coherence and evolution in society.	• Fragmentation, lack of continuity.
• Long-term thinking and planning, commitment, careers for life.	• Constant change. Flexibility. Reluctance to plan or commit long-term in any area of life.
• Structures, organisations, hierarchies.	• Relationships, networks, informality.
• Reality can be grasped by reason.	• Reality is manufactured – image is all.
•Mass production.	• Customisation and consumerism.

This table inevitably oversimplifies what are complex issues and trends on which there is still a lot of discussion. What makes it even messier is that there is no tidy dividing point in time from which this change of paradigm can be dated. Postmodernity is an advancing tide but has not yet swept all before it. Most of us live somewhere between modernity and postmodernity, with a mishmash of attitudes from both.

The generation game

The younger we are, the more 'postmodern' our outlook is likely to be. 'Generation X' is the name given to those born in the 1960s and '70s, who were the first to grow up in an increasingly postmodern world and so the first to demonstrate clearly the changed attitudes and outlook.

> 'Gen X co-habit the environment of their Boomer parents, but interpret it very differently. They accept the surface forms of the culture they have inherited, but divorce these from any assumed inner meaning.'[2]

Those born in the eighties and nineties are often called Generation Y or 'the Millennials' and are seen by many as being 'more X than X' – taking the attitudes and beliefs of postmodernity to greater extremes. American Christian researcher George Barna calls them 'the Mosaic Generation' – non-linear thinkers who cut and paste their beliefs and values from a variety of sources. He describes them as a generation comfortable with contradictions, and says many of them don't know and don't care about moral absolutes.[3]

Whatever disagreements there might be about the finer detail of the 'modern' and 'postmodern' outlooks and generational differences, no one can deny that our lifestyle, culture and values are all undergoing fundamental upheavals. These are vividly reflected in the media and popular culture. For example, a recurrent theme in films over the last twenty years has been to question the nature of reality – *Blade Runner*, *The Matrix* and *The Truman Show* are examples of this.

> Blade Runner, which first appeared in 1981, is widely regarded as a cult postmodern film. In a Los Angeles of the future, artificial humans – 'replicants' – have been created who are almost indistinguishable from real humans. The question of who is real and who is a replicant recurs throughout the film, and by the end is replaced by the question of whether it really matters anyway. The film contains other postmodern themes, such as the pervading atmosphere of gloom and the lack of hope or purpose in the characters.

---

[2] Gerard Kelly, *Get a Grip on the Future Without Losing your Hold on the Past* (London: Monarch, 1999), p.41.

[3] *Assist News*, 5 February 2002.

Style over substance

The primacy of image and style over substance is demonstrated daily in the western press and media. Many 'celebrities' are famous for being famous or connected to those who are famous, and countless pages are written about the latest image change of well-known pop-star, actors, footballers or media personalities.

> The singer Madonna 'is quite consciously all surface, all put-on, all dress-up, all make-over, all simulation … She knows that we live in an age of hype, of hyper-reality. She knows that simulation and appearance mean more than substance and reality. She knows that the appropriation and replication of the original are more real than the original. Thus she is deliberately trivial, shallow, formulaic. And not only in her videos. She realises that "real" life is just showbiz also.'[4]

Christianity in a postmodern era

At first glance, postmodernity can look like bad news for Christianity. A rejection of absolute truth and an acceptance of many equally valid paths are what define a postmodern view of religion and spirituality. On the other hand, in a postmodern world, reason and science are no longer seen as the ultimate guides to truth. There is a recognition that reason alone is inadequate for understanding the world and the meaning of life, and a new openness to faith and spirituality. Modernity tended to

---

[4] Jim Powell, *Postmodernism for Beginners* (London: Writers & Readers, 1998), p.138.

confine spirituality to the narrow domain of the private
life – something for those so inclined but not to be allowed
to pollute the waters of politics and science. In many ways,
postmodernity is responsible for putting spirituality back
on the map and making it acceptable once again in every
area of life.

> 'After years in the popular wilderness, God is staging
> a comeback … Reappraisal for the spiritual life is
> coming from the least likely quarters: scientific,
> secular and popular.'[5]

In many 'Christian' societies however, postmoderns see
Christianity as part of the establishment of modernity that
is being rejected, and so the new openness to all options
for spiritual discovery excludes what the church has to
offer. Religious beliefs in a postmodern world may have
little or no connection with traditional orthodox
Christianity but rather be selected from a smorgasbord of
paganism, New Age thinking, astrology and other world
religions. The new openness to all things spiritual, for
many, excludes Christianity.

Despite this – for the Christian postmodernity opens up
some great new opportunities. It challenges accepted ways
of doing things and encourages initiative and innovation.
It provides a new focus on individuality and customisa-
tion. And the openness of younger generations to all
things spiritual changes the whole environment that we
have been working in for decades. It's no longer a question of persuading people that there is a spiritual side to
life and that they have a God-shaped hole inside them. We

---

[5]   *The Face*, January 1997. Quoted in Gerard Kelly, *How to Get a
Grip*, p.190.

are now faced with presenting our faith as *the* way to know God as Father in a generation that rejects absolutes and prefers the pick 'n' mix approach to spirituality.

Postmodernity – good or bad?

Every human being grows up and lives within a given set of social and cultural circumstances, developing values and an outlook on the world shaped by the prevailing attitudes and norms around them. For those who have grown up steeped in the era of modernity, postmodernity can seem threatening, undermining and even downright evil. To many older people, particularly in the church, the outlook, culture and values of younger generations can seem to be almost anti-Christian. Anti, that is, the particular culture-shaped version of Christianity that they have grown up with and see as right and normal.

In reality, the forms and expression of faith as well as the church structures and worldview in which each of us is steeped are also culture-related. For example, the modern missions movement began in the west in the mood of optimism and purpose created by the Enlightenment in the late eighteenth century. The model around which mission agencies typically ran their operations was that of the trading companies such as the East India Company. This model suited the circumstances of the time, but it had no specific 'biblical' basis. Yet today, many who have grown up with this model would be horrified to see it being questioned and new models being developed.

Similarly, in the late twentieth century the growth of the house church movement and of decentred church networks may be seen in a cultural sense as an expression of the postmodern distaste for structures and hierarchies, as represented by the traditional denominations. Our ways of expressing Christianity are influenced by the culture in which we live, and in fact the 'traditional' ways of doing church and mission in the early twenty-first century owe much to the ideas of modernity.

The optimism and idealism of modernity, combined with a confident belief in the universal truth of the Christian message, fuelled the explosion of western mission to the rest of the world which helped give rise to the global church of today. On the negative side of the scales, it was in essence a very secular and humanist outlook.

● It said that progress was more or less guaranteed, and it was down to human ability only, not God's intervention.

● It undermined the validity of religious faith by setting up human reason as the judge of what was true.

● It confined religion to individuals' private lives.

Though the harmful impact of these elements took decades to work through fully, by the early twentieth century there was a widespread view that religion was irrelevant to the really important issues of public life. Moreover, the American church (and to a lesser extent its British equivalent) had largely polarised into two camps. One saw social transformation as the central mission of the church, to the neglect of conversion and salvation; the other maintained essential Christian truths but '[fled] the problems of the world [in its] fascination with inner spiritual life and the details of end-times prophecy.'[6] The arrival of postmodernity, with its validation of spirituality and experience combined with scepticism about the progress 'myth', has helped to change the nature of the debate and bring the two poles together. People coming from both ends of the spectrum are rediscovering that true spirituality is about both intimacy with God and involvement in his world.

> 'Each generation is called to work out what it means to live for Christ in its own era. But it is not called to make any answer it may find to be normative for all the succeeding generations.'[7]

In short then, history suggests that 'all cultural movements are ambiguous'.[8] Not only does history demonstrate this ambiguity, but the Bible leads us to expect nothing else. Culture is made by people who are themselves made in the image of God, but also exhibit a fallen nature. Our sinfulness doesn't completely erase the fact that we are made in the image of God, but neither does it leave any part of our being untouched. It is often the case that our weaknesses are the flip-side of our strengths, and that many of the evil things we see in our world are a corruption of what is good.

If this is true for humans individually, it is true for us collectively. So the cultures that we create are both good and bad, all mixed up together. Just as you can't easily separate your own strengths from your weaknesses, you also can't easily separate out the good and bad from cultures. So-called 'western individualism' (often criticised) is based on a deep commitment to the value of each person. We may look enviously at societies that are more communal in nature, without realising the social control that goes on in those contexts. In both cases, there are good and bad aspects, the latter being the downside of the former.

---

[6] James F. Engel and William A. Dyrness, *Changing the Mind of Missions* (Downer's Grove, IL: InterVarsity Press, 2000), p.63.

[7] Richard Tiplady, 'Let X=X: Generation X and World Mission', in William D. Taylor (ed.), *Global Missiology for the 21st Century* (Grand Rapids, MI: Baker Academic, 2000), p.472.

[8] Engel and Dyrness, *Changing the Mind*, p.61.

Christians have always had to live and work within their cultural setting and to adjust their strategies accordingly. Aspects of postmodernity may present some new challenges, but to deny that they are happening or simply react against them risks consigning the church and mission to increasing irrelevance. What we need is God-given discernment to distinguish between the essentials of the gospel and the particular strategies and 'containers' by which it is conveyed into our culture.

Summary

❏ From our culture and upbringing, each of us has a lens through which we look at and evaluate the world around us – this is our worldview.

❏ Western culture is moving from 'modernity' (characterised by rationalism, structures, conformity and progress) to 'postmodernity' (emphasising personal experience, relationships and informality, diversity, scepticism).

❏ The growth of a postmodern outlook is having a huge impact on the attitudes and behaviour of non-Christians and Christians alike, and therefore on the church and mission.

❏ From a Christian standpoint both modernity and postmodernity have positive and negative aspects, but neither can be regarded as 'right'.

❏ Christians have always had to adapt their strategies to the prevailing culture.

❏ Without abandoning the essentials of the gospel the western church should adapt its mission strategies to postmodernity and embrace the opportunities it brings.

Whatever we might feel about postmodernity, the stark fact is that it is producing fundamental changes in the way in which we look at the world. The cultural lens – our worldview – through which we evaluate and interact with the world is changing dramatically. Some of these changes make the job of communicating the message of Jesus more complicated – others present wonderful opportunities for us. What we can't ignore is the scale of change and the impact that this is having on the church and on its attitude to global mission.

Questions for discussion

1. Looking back at the table of differences between modernity and postmodernity in this chapter, would you say you are mainly modern, postmodern, a mixture of both, or none of these in your outlook?

2. In what ways can you see the influence of 'modernity' in your own life and environment? Think of your church and your workplace and the way they operate. What do you think is good about modernity in these contexts, and what do you think is bad?

3. To what extent have you and your church, and society in general, accepted the 'modern' view that religion is a private matter?

4. Can you think of ways in which postmodernity has affected your life and outlook, and those of your family, friends, church, etc.?

Further resources on postmodernity

Brian D. McLaren, *A New Kind of Christian* (San Francisco: Jossey-Bass, 2001) – offers a constructive vision of what a postmodern Christian might look like.

Gerard Kelly, *Get a Grip on the Future without Losing your Hold on the Past* (London: Monarch, 1999) – a fascinating and accessible account of how and why today's culture is so very different from what has gone before, with ideas on how to cope with the ever-changing scene.

Jim Powell, *Postmodernism for Beginners* (London: Writers & Readers, 1998) – a readable introduction, in semi-comic-book format, to the philosophy and key thinkers of postmodernism. Includes illustrations of how it has affected contemporary culture.

J. Richard Middleton and Brian J. Walsh, *Truth is Stranger than it Used to be: Biblical Faith in a Postmodern World* (London: SPCK, 1995) – Describes postmodernism and how it differs from modernism, and gives a Christian response.

www.growingupdigital.com – website linked to the book by Don Tapscott, *Growing up Digital: The Rise of the Net Generation* (McGraw Hill, NY: n.p., n.d.), which examines the 'first generation to be bathed in bits since birth'.

3

The Global Church – All Change

Christianity – a truly global religion

Christianity is the religion with by far the largest number of followers worldwide. In 2000 Christians were estimated to form nearly one third of the world's population, with a significant number of members in every continent. Muslims, the next largest religious group, by contrast make up just one fifth of the world population and are largely confined to Africa and Asia. Before getting too euphoric about this it is sobering to note that the number of Muslims is growing at an annual rate of 2.17 per cent compared to the Christian growth rate of 1.43 per cent. It may be happening slowly, but at the current rate, Islam will one day displace Christianity as the world's dominant religion.

The most dynamic growth within Christianity has been within the evangelical and, as part of that, the Pentecostal/charismatic movements. The number of evangelicals grew from 84.5 million (2.8 per cent of the world's population) in 1960 to 420 million (6.9 per cent) in 2000. While in 1900 there were virtually no charismatics (including Pentecostals), there are now estimated to be around 345 million making it the one sector of evangelicalism that has seen significant growth.

World religions in 2000	*Estimated nos. of adherents*
Christian	1,973 m
Muslim	1,279 m
Non-Religious	938 m
Hindu	820 m
Buddhist	400 m
Other (Chinese, traditional ethnic, Jewish, etc.)	654.5 m

A shifting centre of gravity

The overall growth in the world church disguises a remarkable shift in Christianity's centre of gravity. The number of Christians outside the west has grown rapidly in recent decades, with much of that growth happening through the Pentecostal and other charismatic churches. Christians in Africa, Asia and Latin America now comprise almost 60 per cent of the total, which means western Christians have become a minority. The overall growth rate of Christianity may be only 1.5 per cent but what this figure masks is the fact that the church in the West is shrinking and much of the church in the southern hemisphere is experiencing dynamic growth. The following chart illustrates this change in geographical distribution.

> More people attend Anglican churches in Nigeria on a Sunday than in the UK.

Fig. 2: The changing face of the global church

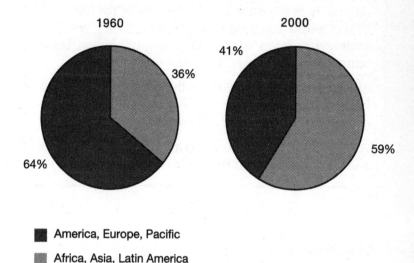

1960

36%

64%

2000

41%

59%

■ America, Europe, Pacific

▨ Africa, Asia, Latin America

Today the church in many countries that received the gospel in the last two centuries is often flourishing and confident, with enormous vitality and evangelistic zeal. Brazil, Argentina, Uganda and some areas of India are just a few examples. Churches in such countries may have little need of western missionaries in their traditional roles of proclaiming the gospel and providing teaching and training in Christian discipleship, because they can do all these themselves. They also have much that they can offer the rest of world.

The church in South Korea

South Korea, with a population of 47 million, has a church that 'was founded on sound indigenous

▶
principles, blessed with a succession of revivals, refined by persecution and is now one of the foremost in the world for missions vision ... Every level of society has been impacted and growth has been remarkable.'[1]

31.7 per cent (16.4 million) of the population claim to be Christian. Of these, the majority (10.6 million) are evangelical, charismatic or Pentecostal.

Around 10,600 South Koreans are engaged in mission work in 156 other countries. (*Operation World*, 2001)

Those of us who live in the UK can develop a distorted view of the place of the church and Christianity in the world. We get used to seeing churches being converted into fashionable apartments, mosques or carpet warehouses. We are regularly bombarded with figures about declining church attendance and become cowed by the constant church-bashing in the media. We have been used to being a Christian country, with basic values and norms grounded in a Christian understanding of the world. We feel under attack from all sides. Although signs of renewed faith and vitality are evident in places, many parts of the church seem to have drawn the wagons round for a long siege and slow slide into irrelevance and extinction.

At the same time there is a tendency for some to mourn the passing of an age when the British Empire was the great torchbearer of Christianity to the ends of the earth. Where once the western church was very definitely the

---

[1] Patrick Johnstone and Jason Mandryk, *Operation World: 21st Century Edition* (Carlisle: Paternoster Lifestyle with WEC International, 2001), p.387.

centre of gravity of world Christianity, creating and controlling international Christian institutions, it is being gradually replaced by the leaders of church movements in places like Africa and Latin America.

So what is our response to these dramatic changes? We are tempted to crawl into our shells, sing our familiar songs and gracefully drop off the map. *'Let's call our missionaries back – after all these new churches don't need our failing version of Christianity any more – they could be of more use here.'* An over-dramatised position this may be but there is no denying the changes that are happening and our need to find a new place within the global church and a new relationship to it.

There are two main reasons for this that we want to explore – firstly, that we have much to gain from the global church in revitalising the church in our own land, and secondly that we have much to give to it. But simply strengthening the worldwide church must not be our aim or the place where we stop. There is an end to which we are called together to work – to see our world reconciled to its Creator and the shalom and justice of the kingdom spreading to every community. When we truly understand that we are part of a global family that contains within it an amazing array of cultures, gifts and richness, we will be able to be open to accepting both all it can offer to us, and all we can contribute to its growth.

Many parts ... one body

The information, communication and travel revolutions that are part of globalisation open up the possibility of Christians from the west and the south relating to each other and working together more closely than ever before, and in new and innovative ways.

Reasons why Western Christians should get involved

... to give

RELIEVING POVERTY AND SUFFERING

1.2 billion people live on less than $1 per day.

150 million children live and/or work on the world's streets.

There are 13 million AIDS orphans in Africa.

In some African countries average life expectancy has dropped from over 60 to as low as 38 – i.e. back to 19th century levels.

WORKING WITH UNREACHED PEOPLES

26.9% of the world population is believed never to have heard the gospel.

Christianity has had no response from some 500 million adherents of traditional religions.

91% of all Christian outreach is in countries where people are already perceived as predominantly Christian.

There are 815 people groups currently without a Christian witness.

77% of those people groups are majority Muslim.

SUPPORTING THE SUFFERING CHURCH

Christians are actively persecuted in 74 countries.

Five of the ten worst countries for persecuting Christians have an Islamic regime, and four have a Communist regime.

Saudi Arabia is the most oppressive to Christians followed by North Korea.

STRENGTHENING NEW CHURCHES

Helping with discipleship, teaching, leadership training and social involvement in places where the church is growing rapidly.

... *to receive*

LEARNING FROM THE FAITH, EXPERIENCE AND EVANGELISTIC ZEAL OF OTHERS

Drawing on the spiritual strengths of Christians in other parts of the world can strengthen the faith and witness of western Christians.

Demonstrating reconcilliation and unity in a world of ethnic and cultural divisions.

ENCOURAGING NOMINAL CHRISTIANS IN THE OLD DENOMINATIONS

The nominal faith of many in the Orthodox, Catholic and some Protestant denominations can be challenged and revitalised through contact with newer Christian groups.

REACHING OUT TO IMMIGRANTS

Most western countries have significant numbers of immigrants of many religious and ethnic backgrounds. Christians from their own or similar backgrounds can contribute to efforts to reach them.

In researching for this book we asked a number of Christian leaders and thinkers of various nationalities to draw on their experience of living in a different culture and pinpoint some of the things that the church in that culture could bring to the global church family. It can be misleading to make broad generalisations, and we need to guard against idealising or over-romanticising Christians of another culture who are as fallible and human as we are. But most of those consulted could almost immediately pinpoint one or two features that were typical of the church in the culture they knew well, and had often radically changed the individual's own outlook. The results are summarised in the diagram below.

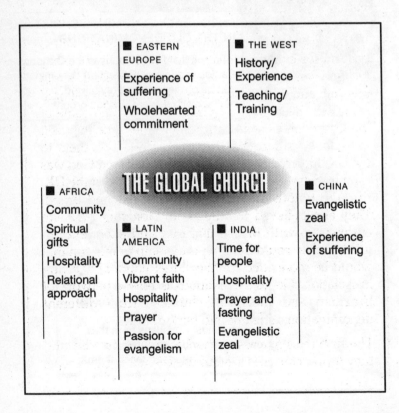

EASTERN EUROPE
Experience of suffering
Wholehearted commitment

THE WEST
History/ Experience
Teaching/ Training

THE GLOBAL CHURCH

AFRICA
Community
Spiritual gifts
Hospitality
Relational approach

LATIN AMERICA
Community
Vibrant faith
Hospitality
Prayer
Passion for evangelism

INDIA
Time for people
Hospitality
Prayer and fasting
Evangelistic zeal

CHINA
Evangelistic zeal
Experience of suffering

There are now over 1,600 missionaries from other nations working in the UK.

How many of us wouldn't welcome into our churches the dynamic faith of Latin America, the evangelistic zeal of Chinese Christians, the understanding of community from Africa? Within the global church all of these are available to us. As one global body we have all the elements we need – they're just not spread very evenly. We haven't yet recognised and taken on the identity and thinking of a global family that would allow us to work effectively together.

Fancy a little Latin passion?

In the early 1990s a network of church leaders with a passion for evangelism came together in Brazil. They felt God was challenging them to get involved in world mission, and to do so through partnership and shared resources. Their original vision was to reach some of the least evangelised countries, but they saw the need to establish a European base, and God drew them to the UK. Inspired by Malachi 4:6 they believed God was calling them back to their 'spiritual fathers' in the UK, through whom the gospel had first reached Brazil. They also believed that by joining together Brazilian enthusiasm with British maturity and experience in mission they could build a partnership in mission that would be more effective than either nationality acting in isolation. Go To The Nations is now a network of Brazilian and European churches from different denominations, streams and backgrounds.

The first missionaries to the UK arrived in 1993 and they found churches around the UK willing to receive them to work in joint ministry within the local church and community. The Brazilians aim to infect UK churches with their passion for relationships, prayer and worship. They have had a remarkable impact in some of the churches they have been attached to. Some of the Brazilians have moved on as missionaries to India, and eastern or western Europe, usually with financial and prayer backing from their UK church as well as their Brazilian church. But GTTN sees the whole mission-building process as long-term.

Visits are also arranged for people from the UK to Brazil to experience the atmosphere, relationships, and love that are part of church life there. Many have returned transformed.

Diversity – 'the divine mosaic'

Diversity – thorn in the flesh or crowning glory?

Communism was intended to bring a unity and togetherness to all people; it insisted that everyone be the same – eat the same food, live in the same houses, have the same lifestyle – unity and community was to come through uniformity.

Unity should not to be confused with uniformity. Christians are called to unity, but not to be the same, to look alike, talk the same way, have the same preferences, see things the same way, come to the same conclusions. God clearly enjoys variety – the Trinity itself bears witness to this, as do the faces of the people around us, the dazzling array of creatures with which we share the planet, the forests, deserts, seas and ice-caps.

Many people tend to think of heaven as being one homogenous lump of people caught up in wonder, love and praise. One of the surprises we may well be in for is the incredible diversity of heaven, with people from every tribe and nation doing their wonder, love and praise in an amazing variety of ways – what a picture! There's a verse in Revelation (Rev. 21:26) that hints at this. Talking about the New Jerusalem, John says 'And all the nations will bring their glory and honour to the city'. Surely one of the glories God created in the nations is the wonderful diversity of cultures and expressions of being human. Maybe part of the glory that each people group brings into heaven will be its own unique expression of its humanness and its creation in the image of God.

> The Gospel's like a seed, and you have to sow it. When you sow the seed of the Gospel in Palestine, a plant that can be called Palestinian Christianity grows. When you sow it in Rome, a plant of Roman Christianity grows. You sow the Gospel in Great Britain and you get British Christianity. The seed of the Gospel is later brought to America, and a plant grows of American Christianity. Now when missionaries came to our lands they brought not only the seed of the Gospel, but their own plant of Christianity, flower pot included! So, what we have to do is to break the flower pot, take out the seed of the Gospel, sow it in our own cultural soil, and let our own version of Christianity grow.[2]

---

[2] D.T. Niles of Sri Lanka, quoted in Paul-Gordon Chandler, *God's Global Mosaic* (Downers Grove, IL: InterVarsity Press, 2000), p.16.

Diversity is a gift of God – something to be celebrated and marvelled at. The church across the world shares one gospel but it finds expression in a myriad of ways as each person's culture and experience lead them to understand it differently and respond in unique ways. God meant us to be united in our diversity – a diversity which itself speaks of the marvellous breadth of his creativity. Diversity is not therefore something to be suppressed to help us be more united but rather something to be celebrated as a gift of God. The uniting factor is God himself and our worship of him as we work out his purpose of reconciliation and unity in the world.

Divided we fall

The Bible makes it clear (for example in John 17) that God wants his people to reflect who he is and be one. We also recognise the wonderful diversity that God has created in the human race and see this reflected in the cultures of the world and the expressions of life and worship in the church. And yet we look at the church in our own land and around the world, and one of the hallmarks seems to be division. Instead of celebrating the diversity, we have used it as reason for staying separate. Instead of focusing on and celebrating the things we hold in common, we have fought and split over the things we disagree on – issues that are so often peripheral rather than central.

Much could be said on this subject and all of us have our own cherished and (to us) important reasons for keeping certain groups at arm's length. There may, however, be only one argument that really counts: what does God think? Does He withhold himself from those we would exclude if we were Him?

Each of us has faults – and yet God seems to have no qualms about working with and through us, especially when we're at our weakest. No church tradition has got it all right – and yet, if we're honest about it, we can see evidence of God graciously at work within every church – however heretical we might feel it to be. Our tendency is to want to oppose and exclude, God's seems to be to want to engage and include.

Summary

❑ There are nearly two billion Christians worldwide, making Christianity by far the largest religion on the planet.

❑ The balance in the Christian world (in numerical terms) has shifted from the west to the south.

❑ The diminishing western church has much to learn from the rapidly developing church in other parts of the world – and much to offer to it.

❑ Unity with diversity is what we should aim for and celebrate.

❑ The first step is to see ourselves as global Christians, part of the global church with a global mission.

The days of mission being 'from the west to the rest' have gone – the global church has grown and matured. The new era we are entering is not, however, simply a reversal of this historical position but a multi-coloured, multi-cultural 'from everywhere to everywhere'. What an opportunity God has given us in the twenty-first century to take the gifts, talents, creativity, diversity from cultures around the world and stitch it into a rich tapestry that can reach into every corner of the world. Excited? We are!

Questions for discussion

1. To what extent do you still see the western church as being the world centre of Christianity? Give reasons for your views.

2. How far is there still a role for mission from the West to other parts of the world?

3. Have you had any contacts with Christians from other countries that have given you new insights or encouragement in your faith? If so, describe what happened.

4. Looking at the diagram on the global church earlier in this chapter, from which of the cultures described do you think you or your church might have most to learn?

Further resources on the global church

Paul-Gordon Chandler, *God's Global Mosaic: What we can Learn from Christians around the World* (Downers Grove, IL: InterVarsity Press, 2000) – considers how different peoples around the world view and worship God; readable and full of thought-provoking stories and insights.

Patrick Johnstone and Jason Mandryk, *Operation World: 21st Century Edition* (Carlisle: Paternoster Lifestyle with WEC International, 2001) – the indispensable guide to the world church, containing facts, figures, comment and prayer pointers.

4

Trend-spotting

Change, change and more change

Chapter 1 explored the ways in which the process of globalisation is changing the way the world works – making us more interconnected and more globally aware. Chapter 2 gave a brief overview of postmodernity and how a whole new mindset and way of seeing the world is developing – particularly in the younger generations. Chapter 3 looked at some of the ways that the global church is changing and the place of the western church within the global whole.

Any one of these changes happening in isolation would be expected to have a significant impact upon the way that the church does and views world mission. The three changes happening at the same time produce a potent cocktail that is set to dramatically reshape the global mission of the church.

At the beginning of the twenty-first century, we stand in a time of transition. The old era of world mission, an era defined and dominated by the mission societies, is coming to an end. A new era is on its way, but it is not yet clear exactly what that new era will look like. This 'paradigm shift' can be a frightening time – a time when old certainties no longer seem to work and trusted methods don't produce the results they once did. A time when people realise that new ways are required but are not sure what those new ways are.

Times of dramatic change can be very threatening – but they are also laden with opportunity. The dawning of a new era opens up new possibilities – the transnational corporations, the big brands, the technically savvy are making the most of them – it's time that the church did too. Faced with change it is too easy to be intimidated and do nothing, or worse, oppose the changes and stay stuck in the past. The alternative is to engage – to get stuck in, to try to steer the changes in positive directions and to use them to demonstrate the love of God to a world in need.

Trend-spotting

Understanding the changes that are happening in the world around us is an essential first step if we are to become salt and light in the new era. Having our finger on the pulse of change helps us to spot the trends that are emerging. In a time of transition, it is these trends that provide clues to what the future is going to look like.

There is already clear evidence of trends emerging that are having a significant impact on world mission. Understanding what the important trends are, what impact they will have and how significant they will be for mission is more an art than a science. Many of the trends are interlinked and reinforce each other and it is hard to view them in isolation. The remainder of this chapter will examine some of these trends and their likely impact.

1. Disintermediation (cutting out the middle-man)

What's happening in the world?
Middle-men have been an integral part of the way the world has always operated. To get 'tea from China' to our breakfast tables has involved producers, packers, shippers, merchants, wholesalers and retailers to name but a few. In a globalised world, however, I can now get on the Internet and have direct and instant communication with primary producers on the other side of the world. I can even order my tea directly from the farm or estate where it is grown. This direct communication and the global mindset that goes with it are beginning to undermine the role of the middle-men – the intermediaries. (The posh word for this trend is therefore disintermediation.)

How is this being reflected in mission?
Many mission agencies have in some important respects been operating as middle-men. Churches have given their money and people to the agencies (the mission professionals) who have then decided how and where to use these resources. Seldom have churches been involved in deciding the mission strategy to which their money and people have been used.

As ordinary people within our churches begin to become more aware of what's going on in the world and travel to other places on business or holiday, so they begin to develop interests and views about global mission.

- We are already seeing many churches making direct contact with a church or project in another country through some personal link.

- Some churches want to have a greater say in where the money they give to an agency will be used and receive reports on progress and success.

- Others want to have a say on the question of which part of the world the people they put forward to agencies will be sent.

- Leaders of churches go and visit their 'missionaries' and get involved in their pastoral care and issues relating to their well-being.

- Individuals who give money want to decide where it will be used and for what type of work. They may want to go and get involved themselves or have direct contact with those benefiting from their gift.

2. Diversity – your way, my way, any way

What's happening in the world?
At the same time as we see the rise of global brands like Coca-Cola and Nike and the development of a dominant global culture, we are also seeing the 'blooming of a thousand flowers'. In a world of so much apparent sameness, people are feeling the need to establish their own identity and uniqueness. This can be seen in the increasing importance of ethnic identity and the rise of religious fundamentalism, both of which reflect people's search for something to belong to, giving them a sense of security and a place in the world.

One of the characteristics of postmoderns is a distrust of any big picture. People's freedom and right to believe what they like are becoming ever more important with the concept of absolute truth being not only alien but offensive. 'If it works for you – do it' is the mantra of postmodern life.

Taken together, these two factors are reflected in a trend of 'anything goes'. In the place of one accepted right approach or way of doing things, the gate is open to lots of different ideas and methods. Instead of uniformity we are seeing diversity.

How is this being reflected in mission?
In the missions arena this is beginning to have an impact.

● If evangelism is your thing – God bless you, get on and be an evangelist. You've got a heart for street kids – great, it's a growing issue that is part of our biblical calling to the orphans and widows. 'I'm passionate about the environment' – fantastic, we need people to help us be good stewards of God's earth.

● Twenty years ago, mission was the preserve of the mission agencies. Nowadays a growing number of churches are getting involved directly in mission in another country – with no mission agency anywhere in sight.

● Christian businesspeople setting up commercial enterprises in other countries are now being accepted as a valuable part of the whole missions effort.

We are seeing, and many are accepting, a much greater diversity of approaches to global mission and types of people involved in mission.

3. Relationships R Us

What's happening in the world?
Amongst the younger generations, one of the most obvious marks of postmodernity is the the importance of personal relationships. Distrust of large structures, big impersonal organisations and hierarchies is an indicator of this move towards the personal. It is another one of those strange ironies of the future that, when impersonal

and instant communication across the world is now possible via email or text message, personal relationships are becoming more important.

How is this being reflected in mission?
For decades mission agencies have received the regular support of churches and individuals and used these as they saw best. Denominational agencies like the Baptist Missionary Society received budgeted annual gifts from just about every Baptist church in the UK affiliated to the Baptist Union.

Figures from Global Connections indicate that overall giving to mission in the UK has remained stable and even grown in recent years. This overall trend, however, masks an important shift in the pattern of giving. Support for individuals, specific projects, and specialist agencies is strong and has in many cases seen a marked growth. General support that agencies use for running costs, over-heads, etc. has shown a marked decline.

In short, people seem happy to give to specific mission activities or people that they have some personal connection to or empathy with. General giving to a favourite agency is in decline, making it a nerve-wracking time for some of the more established missions who have relied for decades on regular contributions from a committed group of churches or individuals.

4. Welcome to the global village

What's happening in the world?
Through globalisation and the resulting changes in the way that the world is working it is becoming harder and harder to live within our own little bubble – untouched by the world around us. Globalisation produces a two-way street

– we influence others and they can influence us – our lives are interconnected and interdependent. Ring a freephone helpline from London and get answered immediately by an Indian sitting in a call centre in Bombay.

How is this being reflected in mission?
Fifty years ago, world mission was simple. Missionaries went from the west to the rest of the world to convert other nations to Christ and bring to them the benefits of modern civilisation like healthcare, water and roads. Since then, life has become far more complicated. Take our own organisation, Oasis Trust, a relatively small agency, as an example. There are British people working in India, Uganda, Zimbabwe and various other countries. There is a Brazilian working in Mozambique, an Indian guy married to a Brit working in Uganda, a Zimbabwean training in the UK. One British guy went to India and married an Indian; they moved to the UK for further training and are now in Bangladesh.

Mission is no longer the 'west to the rest' – it is now coming of age and becoming genuinely everywhere to everywhere. For us in the west this represents a significant adjustment and an exciting opportunity. As we see ourselves as partners with churches and organisations around the world, our mindset will increasingly become one of receiving input from others as well as contributing what we have.

Anny Rosciani from Argentina came to England in 1994 and studied at All Nations Christian College. During a placement at two churches in the Finchley area, she realised how many opportunities there were in London for crosscultural mission. After a year working in Oxford amongst international students she moved back to Finchley in 1999. In 2002

▶

Anny's main role was acting as a link person between
local churches in the area, encouraging and challenging them to reach out to the people of foreign origin
who live in their area, many of whom are Japanese.
Her longer-term vision is to equip Japanese Christians
who are in the UK so that they will evangelise and
disciple other Japanese people when they return
home. Her home church in Argentina has supported
her throughout her time in the UK.

CMS, a mission agency serving Anglican churches
and other denominations, is committed to supporting mission 'from everywhere to everywhere' and is
increasingly recruiting its 'mission partners' from
around the world to work in third countries. For
example, Arun John from north India has been jointly
sponsored by CMS and USPG to work as the parish
priest of Christ the Saviour Church Lenasia, South
Africa since 1997. Mariha Andjelkovic a Serbian agricultural specialist, was sponsored by CMS on a year's
placement in Georgia in 2001–02. She already had significant experience of working with young children,
alcoholics and the homeless. She was active in chari-
table projects run by the local Baptist church and the
local Orthodox church, and also started a Bible-study
group and Sunday school.

5. A bite-size life

What's happening in the world?
Employment patterns have changed dramatically over the
last twenty years. The days of a job for life, staying with

the same company from apprenticeship to retirement, are now very dead. Younger people are far more likely to spend a few years in one place, move on to another firm and then switch careers into something totally different. There is a mobility and short-term mentality about employment with very little sense of loyalty on the part of either the employee or their employer.

People now tend to have a much shorter-term outlook and forward planning is measured in weeks or months rather than years. We want to see visible, definite achievements and undertake projects that have a clear focus and specified closure.

How is this being reflected in mission?
The days of missionaries travelling by ship to start a ten-year assignment from which they might never return, are long past. In mission speak, a two-year commitment used to be considered short-term – nowadays two weeks or two months is short-term and two years considered a long-term commitment.

One phenomenon that accounts for a growing percentage of mission involvement is the gap year. Gap years have become increasingly common with younger people typically having a six-month experience arranged by one of the many mission agencies or church groups that offer this option.

A different part of the same trend is the desire of individuals or churches to get involved in some specific project with clear objectives and a definite end point. Commitment to the general work of an organisation is less and less common, whereas individual or group attachment to some specific place, person or project is growing.

Summary

❑ The world is changing and our attitude towards it is changing.

❑ Certain key trends amongst all these changes are already visible:

Cutting out the middlemen (disintermediation)

Diversity

The importance of relationships

The rise of the global village

A life lived in bite-sized chunks.

❑ These changes are beginning to have an impact on world mission and will dramatically reshape the way the Christian community does mission in the coming decades.

The global trends explored above are producing significant changes for every community – not least the Christian community. It seems that almost every other new Christian book or conference is exploring the future shape and style of the church, desperately seeking new ways of doing and being church. It is hardly surprising therefore that we are beginning to see the first tremors of change rippling through the world mission scene. Nothing short of a massive earthquake is on its way that is going to dramatically alter the landscape of global mission.

Probably the biggest change in the global mission scene will be the new role of the local church in the emerging era. The next chapter focuses on what this all means for churches and begins to explore the new landscape of global mission, with the local church taking a more prominent position. Our core message to every local church is:

> *You can do it! Global mission is your bag – it is a core part of the role of the local church. Explore it and get involved!*

Questions for discussion

1. Do you personally find change threatening or exciting? How does your church react to change?

2. Do you recognise the trends described in this chapter? In what ways are they already visible in your own circumstances?

3. To what extent are you seeing these trends reflected in the mission activities that you or your church are involved in?

4. What about other churches you've heard about?

Resources on trend-spotting

The following books are about discerning future trends in society and/or the church. While they are not concerned to relate these specifically to global mission, the changes they highlight inevitably affect mission, as they do other aspects of church life.

Patrick Dixon, *Futurewise – Six Faces of Global Change* (London: HarperCollins, 1998) – highlights the extraordinary pace at which change is now happening in all areas of life, and predicts some key trends that will in time affect all of us.

Gerard Kelly, *Get a Grip on the Future Without Losing your Hold on the Past* (London: Monarch, 1999).

Michael Moynagh, *Changing World, Changing Church* (London: Monarch, 2001) – a clear and easy-to-read analysis of the fundamental changes occurring in society and the impact they are having on the church; gives practical examples of how churches are reacting and finding new ways to 'do' church.

5

Musical Chairs – Mission in the Twenty-first Century

Churches are doing it for themselves

Many churches are beginning to do their own thing in mission. After years of faithfully sending their dues to their favoured agency, some churches are starting to want more direct involvement in *their* mission programme. They look at the large amount of money going every year from their budget to mission agencies or to support individuals in mission and begin questioning the effectiveness and appropriateness of this way of supporting mission. Congregations contain people who travel widely on business and holiday and are in touch with what's happening around the world. Some people have been on a short-term mission team and developed relationships with local people and a passion for a place, church or project. Others in the congregation were born in another part of the world or have a different ethnic background and an interest in a certain country or region.

A mindset influenced by postmodernity leads people to desire more personal contact and involvement. The technologies and options developing as a result of globalisation make direct contact and personal involvement increasingly possible. The result in many churches has been a reshaping of mission involvement – for some churches this may have happened as an organic shift over time, while for others it may have been more conscious and deliberate.

Emmanuel Church in South Croydon, with around 440 members, has a longstanding tradition of mission support. In the 1980s they rethought their mission strategy and it now has two central strands:

- support for indigenous Christians working within their own culture in countries such as Ukraine and Brazil, with the funding sent via Scripture Union, and

- support for members of their own church who have received their approval for going on long or short term Christian service.

Personal relationships are key to both strands of this strategy. Members of Emmanuel got to know the indigenous workers in various countries before agreeing to support them. Spin-offs from the links have included annual visits by teams from Emmanuel to help in youth camps in Ukraine. Visits by members of the congregation and other ongoing personal links are also central to maintaining congregational interest in those who have been sent out from Emmanuel. The church says that sending their clergy on overseas visits has been their best mission investment, because the clergy capture a vision for mission which benefits the whole congregation.

Clearly people are now the prime focus of Emmanuel's mission activity, and giving tends to focus on those agencies with which 'their' missionaries are working. However the church may also give financial support to other mission agencies if there are members of the congregation willing to champion them individually.

One of the most significant turning points for the UK church in the development of direct church involvement was the fall of the Berlin wall in 1989 and the subsequent opening up of Eastern Europe. Pictures of Romanian orphans living in squalor touched the hearts of British Christians. Enterprising churches realised that they could load a lorry with toys, blankets or food and, in a couple of days, drive it to their chosen location and hand over the goodies themselves. Collections began, volunteers came forward and a whole new area of mission activity opened up almost overnight.

People's experience and opinion of the effectiveness and appropriateness of these efforts varied widely. Some were horrified by this amateur army of new missionaries and point to the cases where inexperience or lack of preparation and research rendered their efforts worthless. For many mission agencies, 'mission' work happening without them, and effort and resources expended on mission not being channelled through them, was a serious shock to the system. Whatever the fruit of those efforts were, for many people and churches, they opened up the Pandora's box of getting directly involved in mission.

Research indicates that this trend is continuing. A growing number of churches from across the denominations are changing their pattern of mission involvement. Almost exclusively this means a growing level of active church engagement in mission. The future is undoubtedly one in which mission will no longer be the sole preserve of the specialist agencies but include churches as significant players.

Christchurch Baptist Church in Welwyn Garden City, with about two hundred members, was helped by Radstock Ministries (see below under 'further resources') to establish a relationship with a church in Albania, and has sent short-term teams there. Because many churches in Albania were only set up after 1989, church leaders there are often rather young in the faith and lacking in many of the resources that are available in the west. Christchurch is therefore supporting a couple from their congregation who will spend about a year in Albania providing guidance and mentoring to the local pastor and his congregation.

No more 'home' and 'away'

It is often said that globalisation is shrinking the world – making it a smaller place. People are becoming increasingly aware of the world beyond their own neighbourhood with international travel becoming more and more common and the media putting us in instant touch with events on the other side of the world. These things are leading to a blurring of the lines between what is considered local and what global. Events on the opposite side of the world can now affect us just as dramatically as if they were down the street.

In the not too distant past the church made a very clear distinction between 'home mission' and 'overseas mission'. Denominations had (and often still have) separate structures and people for their local work and international work. Churches have traditionally put their mission activities in their community into a different box from their involvement in overseas mission. Such a distinction made sense in terms of the way in which the church was involved.

As we begin to take on a global mindset and see ourselves more as global citizens than Londoners or New Yorkers, the distinction between home and away becomes less relevant or meaningful. Some churches are scrapping their missions committee and instead focusing on their involvement in the world – be that locally, nationally or internationally, as one whole.

> Do you still see the world as 'here' and 'abroad'? Does your church still have 'home' and 'oveseas' boxes?

St James, Muswell Hill, is a large Anglican church in a prosperous North London suburb. In addition to its own congregation it also hosts a Spanish-speaking church run by Samuel Cueva, a pastor from Peru. Samuel and his family felt that God called them to serve Him in the UK and came over in the late 1990s. It was apparent chance that brought them to St James initially, but they believed God told them that was where they should start their ministry, and St James agreed.

Although the two congregations meet separately, Samuel is a member of the St James' ministry team and the two congregations cooperate in local evangelism and ministry. Two teams from St James have gone to Samuel's home church in Lima with the aim of strengthening mutual support and fellowship and undertaking joint outreach there.

Is this world mission? If so, who are the missionaries and who the 'mission field'? Such questions are meaningless in these circumstances.

Variety – the spice of life

One of the outcomes of the trends described in Chapter 4 is a growing acceptance of different ways of doing things. In the early twentieth century, people like Henry Ford insisted that there was one right and scientific way of doing things and that we should strive to find it in order to rid the world of uncertainty and mistakes. This understanding epitomises the 'modern' mindset. Postmodernity reacts forcefully against this way of thinking, recognising that there is often no one right answer and that diversity is to be welcomed not eliminated.

We've been talking to churches up and down the UK uncovering how some of them are getting more involved in global mission. One of the exciting things about this has been to discover the vast range of approaches people are taking.

St John the Evangelist, Blackheath (C of E), decided to tithe the money it raised to refurbish its church building and use the money on a building project in a poorer country. This led to their helping to build a cathedral for the Tanzanian diocese of Mara and active involvement in a range of other projects as well as Bible teaching within the diocese.

St Luke's, Formby (C of E), supported missionaries in Rwanda for about fifty years. However its direct relationship with a church there began when a member of the St Luke's congregation visited in 2001 as part of a group organised by a mission agency.

A couple from *Brighton Road Baptist Church, Horsham,* worked in Kenya for several years. The Horsham church supports a pastor that the couple had worked with and arranged for him to visit the UK for six weeks in 2002, where he had a big impact on church members of all ages.

One member of Brighton Road Baptist in Horsham started a foster home in Romania for around twelve children with HIV/AIDS. Another member of the same church started another foster home in the same area for children with disabilities. The church provides the main funding to keep both homes going, and church members of all ages visit regularly to help there.

Carshalton Beeches Baptist Church is helping to build a church for a congregation in Romania. Members of the church regularly go out to help with the construction and to provide preaching and teaching for the local congregation.

In 2000 Carshalton Beeches Baptist also ran a Millennium Missions Project to raise £10,000, which was shared between four separate projects aimed at unreached peoples and run by four different mission agencies in four different geographical areas. A couple from the church then went to work in a country where one of the unreached people groups lived.

St Mary's Church, Goudhurst (C of E), has had a link with the Theological College of Lanka, Sri Lanka, and with several parishes there, since 1986. As a result of visits made in both directions, friendships have been built and financial support given from time to time for several projects in Sri Lanka.

One size does not fit all! There is no one recipe for your church to get involved in global mission – you are free to plough your own furrow – to do what comes naturally to you. Diversity is the name of the game – where will you start?

A holistic approach

For many older people or those with a more traditional evangelical outlook, mission – real mission – is about evangelism and its sister, church planting. These activities are seen as primary with other, more social action-oriented initiatives being put into a less important (and less Christian) 'charity' bracket. In many ways this reflects a 'modern' outlook on the world that divides the sacred from the secular.

Throughout this book, the term 'mission' is used in the widest possible sense as an inclusive term covering the vast range of activities undertaken by Christians around the world as they seek to express and demonstrate the love of God. This holistic approach to mission seems to be instinctive to most postmoderns. For many churches that have started their own global mission links and projects, a major motivation has been a wish to do something about poverty, material need, and human suffering. Churches that hold on to a dualistic approach to mission and focus exclusively on evangelism, may find it hard to enthuse and engage younger generations in their missions programme.

Is your view of mission and your church's engagement in global mission, holistic?

Organic is good for you

Many of the churches that have already begun to get involved directly have done so as a result of some personal relationship or contact. Someone from the church may have visited a church in a different country, have a church member working there or hosted a visit by someone from that place. A relationship has developed and grown, people have become friends and quite naturally, without any deliberate strategy, a partnership has been established. Visits in both directions are made, joint projects undertaken, funds made available. The relationship has developed organically with ideas and projects cropping up along the way. Some things don't work, expectations may vary – all natural parts of a developing relationship.

Altrincham Baptist Church (ABC) has about 1,000 attenders. Its links with Jinja in Uganda began after Roger Sutton, the Minister of ABC, heard God tell him in the late 1990s to go to Uganda and take a team. Building on an existing friendship with a Ugandan church leader in Jinja, he led the first team of about twenty ABC members in February 2000. The whole enterprise subsequently grew exponentially, though not without difficult times along the way. Other Baptist churches in the UK have also joined its work in and around Jinja, which includes a sponsorship scheme to enable AIDS orphans to attend a vocational training centre and the establishment of preventative medical health care programmes, as well as teaching and ministry.

Out of this relationship between Christians in Altrincham and Jinja have grown even broader links between the two communities. A 'twinning' link between Jinja and the Metropolitan Borough of

Trafford has been brokered and this relationship is now seen as one of the best and most active twinning links in the UK. A Trafford-Jinja Friendship Association has also been formed and links have been established between schools in Trafford and Jinja.

The link has also helped outreach by ABC in its local area. Members of ABC who have gone to Uganda have been profoundly affected by the experience, and it has given them good opportunities to talk about their faith to non-Christian friends and colleagues. The work the church has put into the link and the way it has spread to the wider community have added to ABC's credibility within that community and with Trafford council.

In this new era of global mission, there are no prescribed starting points and no predetermined paths to follow. The only starting point for you and your church is where you are right now. You may want to develop a strategy to help guide you forward. You may simply want to ask: 'what is the next sensible, manageable step that we can take?' and allow things to develop organically.

Short-term is not a cop-out

For some mission agencies a short-term commitment is still two years – in their view, real missionaries go to the 'field' for a minimum of ten, fifteen or twenty. Some people – mostly from the older generations – are very sceptical of whether anything of value can be achieved in just a few months or even a few years. Fifty years ago, missionaries went to another part of the world, committing themselves to a particular country and location for a significant period of time. The reasoning was that it takes five years to learn a language properly and nearer ten to really understand a different culture and be effective in communicating to it. With this basic pattern as the norm for missionary service, it is easy to see why such people are sceptical of those who turn up for a few months or a couple of years: *'Whilst they may gain some rudimentary language skills, they won't be able to communicate in the people's mother tongue. They may be able to understand some basics of culture, but in their rush to achieve something in their short term of service, they are likely to make some real cultural boobs.'*

People who hold this view of the new trend to short-term mission involvement do have a point. The commitment shown by people spending the best part of their adult lives serving one people was truly awe-inspiring. Indeed, to become so immersed in a culture that one can really understand it and communicate effectively in it does take decades. Most short-term mission work however operates on a different understanding of the role of those who go into another culture. Most people are realistic enough to know that they are not going to get immersed in the culture in order to become like a native. The roles and expectations of people living cross-culturally have changed. Nowadays people tend to go for a specific job – to have some technical or professional input to a larger work alongside local Christians. They may build relationships with local people, they may even be involved in activities that could be labelled 'evangelism', but they do not imagine themselves staying for years and being the primary players in outreach and discipleship – that's the job of the local church and local Christians. Those coming in from the outside come to complement and add to long-term work, not to do it all themselves.

Oasis Global Action sends people from the UK to work on five continents of the world. A vast array of options is available in order to enable people to use the time they can make available and the talents they have.

Oasis's growing work in Uganda is a case in point. Long-term staff from the UK work with Ugandan partners to run a programme for street girls. These two groups provide a continuity and strategy for the long-term development of this work. Other people with specific skills come for a few months to work as a planned part of the wider programme. Young people on gap year programmes get involved, running specific parts of the programme, like sports sessions. Other teams come for just a few weeks and undertake a specific activity like painting a building or running a holiday camp.

The programme is set up in a way that enables each group, with the time and skills they have, to make a meaningful contribution to a planned, long-term programme.

Most mission agencies have accepted that things have changed and have embraced the trend to short-term mission involvement. They try to ensure that people involved for a few months or weeks or years become part of an established programme with long-term aims. If short-termers simply fly in to a place, make a quick splash and then jet off, they are likely to do more harm than good. If however, they come into a situation where their input is a planned part of a bigger programme, then they can make a lasting and positive impact.

So far we have looked at this issue from only one angle – what the people who go are able to give. There is though another side to the coin that is equally important – what do those who go learn and bring back? Oasis has been sending short-term teams since 1991 and now has a vast range of different options – from two weeks to ten months, in teams or on individual placements. Most people who go feel a call from God to be involved in another part of the world. They want to make a difference and really contribute something to the people they are going to serve. The reality however is that the greatest change that takes place is actually in the lives of those who go. Living in a different culture, having to depend on God in a whole new way, the stresses and joys of living in a team environment – all of these things produce profound change. People who go, come back different.

Some people argue that the cost of sending people to another part of the world to contribute relatively little cannot be justified – the money could be used much better locally rather than being given to airlines. This is an understandable reaction – especially from those living and working in poorer countries for whom a typical international airfare represents many years of salary. There is another side to the argument and one that stacks up even from a purely financial perspective. For the vast majority of people who go, even for just a few weeks, the experience radically changes their attitude, understanding and giving to mission. From a financial point of view their giving to mission over the remainder of their lives is likely to increase way over the amount that they spent on their own mission experience. Being realistic, we have also to recognise that much of the money given to individuals to go on a mission experience would not otherwise be given – it is not being diverted from other mission activities – it is new money into the mission pot.

Part of even the briefest mission experience (if it is well set up) is what is given, and often a bigger part, what is learnt. In the same way, half of a short mission experience is going – the other half is coming back. People returning from a mission trip tend to come back fired up with what they have seen and learnt. Those of us in the churches they return to need to see these people as an amazing God-given resource. We have so much to learn from the church and situations in other parts of the world. These people who return to us can bring back insights and experiences that can transform our churches – if we let them.

> Have you ever thought about going? How about taking a team from your church?

Turning the tables – mission agencies are there to help you (not vice versa!)

> Early in 2002 Paul McKaughan, President of the US Evangelical Fellowship of Mission Agencies, was quoted as follows: 'I don't know of any time in my 35 years of mission experience that I have seen or felt mission executives more ready and willing to change and adapt. At the same time, I also don't know of any period in my career that there is less certainty about what changes to make… We know (the future) will be greatly different but are not sure in which ways it will be different… In many ways our strategies and way of thinking do not fit our present reality very well.'

The era of world mission that is passing was the era of the mission society (or agency as they have become known more recently). They were the principal and sometimes only actors in the development of world mission over the last two hundred years. The fact that today one third of humanity owns the Christian faith, and that there are Christians in every nation, is in very large part due to the achievements of the mission societies.

So, given the success, expertise and professionalism of the mission agencies shouldn't we just leave them to it – aren't they God's ordained and only way of undertaking world mission? There are some who would argue that this is the case – the way God has blessed their efforts is his stamp of approval and they should remain as the professionals, encouraged and supported by the rest of the church. Some people have sought justification for the development of mission societies from Scripture, citing the creation of small teams sent out without the oversight of any one church. In fact, as we have seen, mission societies were originally developed as a pragmatic creation to undertake world mission in a way suited the circumstances of the day.

On the other side there are those who would argue, again from Scripture, that world mission is the job of the local church. They point to the fact that much of the development of the early church occurred as people were sent out from one church to plant new churches in other places.

In reality, God seems to allow His people to use whatever structures make sense and work in their context. God's attitude seems to be – 'if it works, go for it!' It is not a question of 'either/or', but 'both … and'.

Many of the trends of the new era in mission that we explored in Chapter 4 seem to be changing the mission agencies' role as the central and essential player in world mission. The agencies themselves are experiencing big changes as they struggle to gain support from younger generations and as churches want to get more involved in mission themselves. There is a recognition in the missions community that massive changes are taking place and most agencies are seeking to understand what's going on and work out their response to it. It is a difficult and unsettling time for many mission organisations and a wide variety of responses are emerging. Some are closing, others looking at mergers, many restructuring, but change is definitely in the air.

The key issue for mission agencies is to find their new and appropriate place within the new world of global mission. Rather than opposing the changes that are happening and trying to cling on to the methods of their heyday, agencies need to engage with the new and embrace the changes taking place and the opportunities that these present. The thought of churches getting directly involved in mission may fill some traditional missions with horror and most people can cite instances when such linkages have gone horribly wrong. The fact is however, that in a globalised, postmodern world, churches are going to get stuck in themselves and mission agencies need to find ways of coming alongside to guide and encourage – but not seek to control.

Three basic models for the role of mission agencies in their relationship with local churches seem to be arising:

1. *Contractor.* The agency continues to be the prime actor in certain mission activities but undertakes these on behalf of the church. Local churches become more involved in thinking about strategy and the placement of resources, but the work is undertaken by the agency.

2. *Partner.* A local church wishing to undertake a particular mission activity works jointly with an agency (or a number of agencies) using the strengths of each. The relationship in terms of decision-making is one of equality and partnership.

3. *Consultant.* A local church doing its own mission activities realises that it needs expert help in a certain area. It contacts an appropriate agency and uses them as a Consultant to provide this expertise.

These three models of engagement between local churches and mission agencies are in one sense all points on a spectrum of options. At one end the mission agency does all the work and makes all the decisions and the role of the church is as passive supporter. This is effectively what the relationship has been in the paradigm we are leaving. At the other end of the spectrum, local churches make all the decisions and do all the work and the mission agencies have no involvement. Neither end of the spectrum makes much sense in this day and age. What needs to happen is for churches and agencies to work together to bring the resources, interests and expertise of each for the greatest impact in global mission. Some churches may feel more comfortable with less direct involvement, whilst others may want to take a much greater role. The onus is on the agencies to adapt their strategies and structures to enable varying levels of involvement by local churches.

It would be a tragedy if churches and businesses getting involved themselves in global mission decided simply to go it alone. Mission agencies are a fantastic source of expertise, advice and encouragement and both sides need to find constructive ways of working together to make the most of the new opportunities.

Church and agency working in partnership

Jim and Jane Currell worked for Oasis in India supported by their home church – St John's, Tunbridge Wells. Following two years training at All Nations Christian College, they began to look at options for a new placement. The Currells themselves, St John's and Oasis looked at the opportunities and together felt God was leading them in the direction of Mozambique. Jim and two members of the church

▶

visited to assess the situation and together all three parties decided this was the right way forward. In April 2002, the Currells moved to Beira in Mozambique.

As a result of the links between Altrincham Baptist Church and Jinja, a member of ABC felt called to full-time Christian work in Uganda, and ABC asked BMS if they could go under its auspices. At that time BMS did not work in Uganda, but – because of this and similar requests from other Baptist churches – it agreed to start working in Uganda.

Here are some of the main services mission agencies can offer, which few churches could provide for themselves:

- Specialist knowledge of other countries and cultures
- Experience of what's involved in sending and supporting people overseas
- Training facilities to prepare prospective mission workers
- Networks and contacts
- Ability to undertake specialised work such as Bible translation

Bible translation – a job for life?

At first glance, you would think that the translation of the Bible into a new language would require workers prepared to commit to the work for decades. Wycliffe Bible Translators is an international family of organisations which provides staff (both westerners and others) to work on projects to translate the Bible into languages where it is not otherwise available.

They have however recognised the postmodern reluctance to make a lifelong commitment and modified their approach accordingly. Under their previous training programme it would have taken one to four years before a recruit made it to the field. But the UK training approach has recently been remodelled to make it modular. Now most recruits join for a fixed term, which they may later decide to renew. A specific field assignment is agreed for each recruit on joining. They take only those modules which are relevant to that assignment, which means they can start working in the field much earlier than before.

Summary

❑ Local churches will become increasingly important in global mission.

❑ The distinction between 'home' and 'overseas' is becoming meaningless.

❑ Mission is becoming more varied, holistic and spontaneous.

▶

❏ Short-term mission can have a real value as part of
an ongoing project or strategy.

❏ Mission agencies have a huge amount of expertise
that could help local churches do mission well.

❏ Local churches can do it! *You* can do it! Global mission is coming within reach of every local church.

Global mission is in a time of rapid and extensive change.
For those who have been at the heart of the 'traditional'
mission movement, these are threatening times. For the
newcomers to global mission a world of new opportunities is opening up, with the promise of a whole host of
ways to become directly involved in global mission.

The local church will be a key player in the future of
global mission and every local church has some valid role
to play – things to bring to the party and things to learn. It
may seem daunting but it is not rocket science – *you* can
do it! Inevitably many people are unsure of where to start
and how to move forward. The last three chapters of this
book are designed to help you begin to move your church
into this brave new world of global mission.

Questions for discussion

1. How would you feel if your church wanted to get
   directly involved in some form of mission? What sort of
   mission work would appeal to you?

2. Does your church – or do members of your congregation
   – have any existing links with Christians in another
   country on which a stronger relationship could be built?

3. Do you think short-term mission experiences (whether for two weeks or six months) have any value? Explain your answer.

4. What roles do you think mission agencies should have in global mission in the twenty-first century?

Resources on short-term mission

Cathie Bartlam (ed.), *Mind the Gap – True Stories of Year-out Projects* (Milton Keynes: Scripture Union, 1999).

Ditch Townsend, *Stop, Check, Go – A Practical Guide for Cross-cultural Teamwork* (Carlisle: OM Publishing, 1996) – written for people planning to go on short-term (i.e. several weeks or months) team trips, it contains practical information and advice.

Crossing Frontiers, produced by the Commonwealth Youth Exchange Council in partnership with Christian Aid, is a pack of ideas to help prepare a group of young adults for a short overseas trip – available from Christian Aid.

Global Connections Code of Best Practice in Short-Term Mission outlines the issues anyone setting up any kind of limited-term mission involvement needs to address. Available from Global Connections, Whitefield House, 186 Kennington Park Road, London SE11 4BT. Tel: 020 7207 2156. Email: info@globalconnections.co.uk.

Radstock Ministries exists to help local churches become directly involved in mission. They help UK churches to set up partnerships with churches in eastern Europe.

Radstock Ministries
2a Argyle Street,
Mexborough
South Yorkshire
S64 9BW
Tel: 01709 582345
Website: www.radstock.org
Email: info@radstock.org

6

Becoming a Global Family

How do we do unity with diversity?

We live in a world and at a time when we are more joined up and conscious of one another than ever before. At the same time as seeing the development of one global economy and global megabrands, we are witnessing the growth of cultural diversity and the search for unique identity. For the worldwide body of Christ, real global unity is now more of a possibility than it has ever been. The church has spread to every nation and we see an amazing 'divine mosaic' of expression of the gospel, each part with its unique and vital contribution to make to the whole. So how do we begin to take up the challenge for the church to work together as the greatest global network the world has ever seen, united in its purpose of building the kingdom of God?

1. Focus on purpose

Firstly, we need to focus on purpose not doctrine. Our tendency for too long has been to place too much emphasis on what is said and the finer details of belief, rather than on what is done. Jesus said many amazing and important things, but rehearse to yourself what the gospel is all about and you'll find that what dominates are the things that he *did*. He came to earth, lived amongst us, healed the sick, died on the cross, rose from the dead and ascended into heaven. Time and again the Bible reminds us that actions speak louder than words and yet it is the words and the thinking that lies behind them that we have given pride of place to. Preaching a good sermon has become more important than feeding the hungry, freeing the oppressed, being activists in God's world. This is what Jesus was going on about in Matthew 25 when he spoke of the sheep and the goats. What does he tell us is the thing that differentiated the two groups? It wasn't what they did or did not **believe**, but what they did or did not **do** when faced with the hungry, homeless, naked.

None of this is saying that belief, doctrine and words are not important – they are. But as human beings of limited intelligence and finite understanding we will only ever be able to grope our way towards the truth. We need to be intimate with God and involved in his world – that is biblical spirituality. We need to be united in working with others who also love Jesus and are committed to serving him, without requiring that they agree with us on every issue of faith and doctrine.

On the surface it would seem that united in purpose should be a lot easier than united in doctrine. But try to begin articulating the details of the purpose that God has given us and the disagreements will once again begin to flow. *'Evangelism is primary!'* *'No, we are called first to show God's compassion in practical ways.'*

The truth once again is that God values and inspires his people to a whole breadth of different activities. Evangelism, relief, development, compassion, etc. are all parts of a whole and it is our different cultures, background, theology and experience that make us believe one to be better than another. We need to take an inclusive approach, rather than seeking to justify our preferences over those of another person or group. We can either let the differences and diversity divide us or embrace them as they bring strength to the whole body and we learn from and complement one another. We do have a common purpose in loving God and loving our neighbour. We are all called to be ambassadors with a message to tell and loving acts of service to do. For some their primary focus will be on telling others about the eternal life available through Christ. For others it will be in acts of service that make God's love real and tangible. Why do we need to say that our preference is better than someone else's? We are all pointing the way to the same God who loves us and wants the best for us throughout eternity.

The key issue is for us to commit ourselves to working together for God's glory and the growth of his kingdom. Our unity and calling to a common purpose are more important than our differences in doctrine. What kind of army is it, engaged in a battle, with a clear job to do, that holds up progress because one section take showers and another baths and they refuse to work together because of it? Let's face it, when our differences in emphasis and doctrine become divisive and stop us working together, it's because we have not grasped the importance and urgency of the task God has given us. When we have time and energy to fight over petty differences whilst the world we are called to reach slides into oblivion, we have taken our eye off the ball in a way that must make God weep.

2. Taking on a global identity

As you've probably gathered by now, there is an unparalleled opportunity for the church arising from the changes taking place in our world. The technology and mindset of a globalised world make it possible for the first time for the church to come together as the greatest global network imaginable. As a global church we can use our diverse talents to strengthen each other and together to bring God's kingdom into every corner of the world and into every human problem.

Being global Christians

The first step along this road is to begin to see ourselves as global Christians. Involvement in our local community – with the people we work with, our neighbours, etc., is a basic building block of the Christian life. We have been encouraged to 'Think Global, Act Local'. But in a world where we are daily impacted by and influence the lives of people around the world, we have to begin to grapple with our global identity. Perhaps 'Think Global, Act Global' is more apt for today?

As the world becomes more interdependent and interconnected, so our actions and decisions in one small corner can send ripples around the world. Our purchasing habits are an obvious example. Each of us tends to buy our clothes according to what they look like and how much we can afford. An issue that rarely enters our head is where this garment has come from, who has produced it and in what conditions have they been working? Or how about timber for the DIY enthusiast: we look at the grain, how straight it is – but has this timber come from a forest being managed in a sustainable way? Is my purchase going to be joining forces with the exploiters and reinforcing a system of oppression, environmental degradation and poverty? Is it going to contribute to and encourage further degradation of the environment? We may not want to ask these questions when we're simply buying a new shirt or shelf, but in our joined-up, globalised world the impact of decisions for good or ill is very real.

Becoming a Global Christian
Some practical ideas to get you thinking

Buy fairly traded products that ensure producers get a decent slice.

Read the world news and pray for world leaders (1 Timothy 2:1,2).

Campaign for trade justice. Raise awareness in your church and write to your MP.

Encourage people you know who are actively involved in mission, by writing or visiting as well as praying

Give of your time and skills. Take a few weeks or months out to use them in a place where they can make a difference. Contact Oasis Trust or Tearfund for ideas. How about tithing your holidays?

Buy a copy of the *Good Shopping Guide* and consult it when you are going to buy something.

Get involved in supporting a project, church or organisation working in another part of the world. Have regular contact, be supportive of staff, go visit – make it part of your life.

Buy *Operation World* and read it, either systematically or to learn and pray about countries in which you have an interest.

Consider working with a Christian mission organisation in the UK, either paid or as a volunteer.

If you travel abroad on business or holiday, find out about the church in the places you visit and see what you could do to help them

Where are you investing your money? Look at bank accounts, savings and shares – could you find a more ethical home for them?

Questions of lifestyle have always been with us, periodically making the top of the pile with the publication of a book like Ronald Sider's *Rich Christians in an Age of Hunger*. For many of us challenges to our lifestyle come onto our radar screen every now and again and prompt a rethink. We may make some adjustments, change some detail of our life but ultimately we're left with a residue of guilt. Yes we know we should try harder, be more conscientious – after all most of us do actually want to do the right thing in terms of lifestyle.

Understanding ourselves as global citizens, having a global identity, is about lifestyle – but it's also much broader than that. At its core, it is about seeing ourselves in a global context, being affected by and influencing the rest of the world. It is about opening up our horizons so that we live out our lives conscious not only of the world immediately outside our front door, but also of what's happening on the other side of the planet. We pray for the family next door and also for our national leaders and world leaders. We keep in touch with what's going on in our local community and what's happening around the world. We make a commitment to be involved in God's world, whether that's volunteering at the local school or praying for, giving to and going to visit Christian work in Bolivia, Burundi or Burma.

Most people, it seems, do actually sign up to the idea of global citizenship and a global identity. The issue is more often the practical reality of living it than any difficulty in accepting the concept. What most of us need are some stories of what other people have done to fire our imaginations – some practical ideas that can put some flesh on the bones. If this is you – watch out for another Connect! book about global lifestyles.

Being a global church

The fact is that we are a global church – we are the greatest global movement the world has ever seen. The problem is that most of us have not recognised this reality, taken on the identity and begun to explore what this means and the opportunities it offers to us. There are some who have begun this journey – Chapter 8 gives some examples of what they are doing. But for most of us, whilst we assent to some concept of the Body of Christ around the world, we have not even begun to let this impact the way we live and 'do' church.

For us in the church, God intends our unity to arise from our common relationship with him – being his children and his people. In 1 Peter 2:9–10, we read the familiar words about God's people being a royal priesthood. Peter is referring back to the message God gave Moses for the people of Israel in Exodus 19. In verse 6 the Lord says, 'you will be for me a kingdom of priests and a holy nation'. Priests were seen as the people who prayed and taught – God's advocates and mouthpiece to the world. So what does that make a nation of priests? Are they simply meant to teach each other? This was the foundation of Israel as a missionary people – God's light to the rest of the world – a whole nation of worshippers and advocates.

In applying the role of God's priests to the New Testament church, Peter is helping us to see that it is our role to be priests in the world – the people who are God's representatives and advocates, who inherit the missionary calling of the people of Israel. We are to be priests to all nations – our calling is a global one. Two questions arise:

1. What does it mean for my local church to have a global identity?

2. How can the church, worldwide, begin to grow into being the greatest global network that has ever existed?

In some ways the rest of this book is trying to work towards answering these two questions. Very often the thing that holds us back is not the desire to do or become something but the imagination and ideas to begin to envisage what we might do.

Just imagine what your church would be like if it had taken hold of its global identity and the church worldwide was really acting as one multi-faceted, joined up, coherent, united, diverse global body.

● Where would your church leader come from? – Brazil, Uganda, India, Clapham?

● What would you pray about during your intercessions?

● How would you be keeping in touch with the four churches around the world that you have specific links with?

● How many members of your congregation will be travelling to visit, learn from and work in your partner churches this year?

● How many visitors will you be receiving from other countries during the year?

● What is the latest issue that your Global Issues Committee is presenting to the church, and asking you to pray for and campaign on?

● How many people in the church wrote to and met their MP during the last campaign?

● How much profit did the Fair Trade stall (in the church hall every Sunday and delivers big orders to your door during the week) make last year? Where did you decide to invest this profit?

● Have you scraped yourself off the ceiling yet after the visit of the Argentinian pastor to your church weekend?

● What plans do you have for growing the capacity of your church buildings to accommodate the Chinese congregation?

3. Working together

The bottom line is that we need each other – we like to think we don't, but we're wrong. None of us on our own can understand it all, be it all, do it all – God deliberately made us interdependent. On our own we will only ever have part of the whole – part of the truth. Embedded in God's design of the human race is our need for community, for sharing, for working together. Take God's people from every tribe and nation and mould them together and you get a wonderful rainbow of gifts, creativity, understanding, perspective. In fact what you get is all that is needed to bring God's kingdom to every corner of the planet and into every human problem.

Summary

❏ The global church is the greatest global network that has ever existed.

❏ If we are to grow into this reality we need to focus primarily on the purpose to which we are called, in order to work with other Christians.

❏ We should become global Christians who are part of a global church.

❏ As individuals this means adopting a global lifestyle and being concerned and involved in what happens in the wider world.

▶

▶

❑ As a church this means sharing what we have and receiving what we lack. We need what Christians from other parts of the world can bring.

To begin to fit into the clothes of the greatest global network, we have to start working together. Despite the ambiguities, the differences in culture or doctrine, we have to affirm that we want to go down this global road and start taking the first steps along it. What we most need as we do this are guidelines to give us some direction and standards to follow, and some principles to help us engage with our brothers and sisters in other parts of the world.

Enter the Connect! Covenant ...

Questions for discussion

1. How good is your church at expressing real unity with other churches in your neighbourhood?

2. In what ways do you find diversity and differences threatening? How might you be able to overcome your fears and be more open to a wider range of people, ideas, etc.?

3. In what ways could you change your lifestyle to be more appropriate for a global age?

4. In what ways does your church already have a global identity? What things could you do immediately to develop the feeling of belonging to a global family?

Further resources on becoming a global family

Ronald J. Sider, *Rich Christians in an Age of Hunger* (Nashville: Word Publishing, 1997).

Charlotte Mulvey (ed.), *The Good Shopping Guide* (N.p.: Ethical Marketing Group, n.d.).

Patrick Johnstone, *Operation World* (Carlisle: Paternoster Lifestyle, 2002).

Steve Chalke and Simon Johnston, *Intimacy and Involvement – How Authentic Christianity can Transform Society* (Eastbourne: Kingsway Publications, 2003) – explores how biblical models of spirituality combined intimacy with God with involvement in the community.

www.ethical-junction.org – a website guide to finding a range of ethical products and services.

7

The Connect! Covenant

By way of introduction to this chapter, let's review the argument so far. The world is changing, our attitude to the world is changing and the whole balance of world Christianity is changing too. These changes are beginning to have a massive impact on world mission, opening up new opportunities for every Christian and every local church to play a part. In order to make the most of these opportunities, the global church needs to begin to see itself and operate as the amazing global network that it is. But how can we do this? How can we overcome the obstacles and differences that hold us back and stop Christians in different parts of the world joining in meaningful partnerships with one another?

Each of us – each person, each church, each part of God's global family – has something of value to contribute to the global mission God has called us all to be part of. For many of us this is scary territory – we believe the theory is right but where on earth do we start? The Connect! Covenant is intended to be part of the answer.

The Lausanne Covenant

In 1974, 2,300 evangelical leaders and theologians from over 150 countries met in Lausanne, Switzerland. Together they developed the Lausanne Covenant – a commitment to work together to evangelise the world, setting out the scope of this work in terms of both evangelism and compassion ministries.

The Lausanne Covenant was a vital step forward in articulating God's calling of the whole church to mission. It spelled out the broad scope of Christian mission and presented a clear doctrine that a huge variety of churches and organisations have been able to sign. The development of the Lausanne Covenant was a fantastic achievement and a massive breakthrough in terms of evangelicals working together and deciding that a whole gospel needed social action as well as evangelism. Getting 2,300 leaders from 150 nations to one place to agree on so much was a miracle!

> **THE LAUSANNE COVENANT**
>
> Lausanne believes...
> - that cooperation and sharing in world evangelisation is better than competition;
> - that the whole gospel will include demonstration by deeds as well as proclamation by words;
> - that biblical theology and mission strategy must be consistent.
>
> The Conclusion of the Covenant states:
>
> Therefore, in the light of this our faith and our resolve, we enter into a solemn covenant with God and with each other, to pray, to plan and to work together for the evangelisation of the whole world. We call upon others to join us.

Taking the next step

Lausanne laid the ground for working together – it was intended as a basis for common action. It was hoped that by articulating a clear doctrine and setting out a clear mandate for Christian mission, people across the world would get better at working together.

We believe that it is time for a new covenant for a globalised era. The purpose of the Connect! Covenant is to help Christians, churches and organisations from different parts of the world to work together. Rather than setting out the common ground of belief from which we can agree to talk together, it will establish the principles under which we agree to work together. It will be focused on facilitating joint action, providing the foundations of a commitment made by people from different cultures and worldviews to help them link up and be effective in what they choose to do.

Instead of being a statement of belief from which action might spring, it should be a commitment to work together, laying principles around which churches from different parts of the world can cooperate and strengthen one another. Instead of being a covenant of common doctrine it should be a covenant that enables action.

How will the Connect! Covenant be built?

In building the Connect! Covenant the temptation is to follow a similar path to Lausanne and physically bring together a broad spectrum of people. But who would come? The big names, the leaders, the theologians – all respected people with much to contribute. But this is not 1974. We live in an age of global communication. Access to the Internet is available in every country and is spreading to even the remotest places. Instead of being developed by a group of theologians, the Covenant should be built by ordinary Christians and church leaders from across the world – people rooted firmly in their local communities and in the practical realities of ministering to a world in need.

The Connect! Covenant is intended to be a tool for use by ordinary people in every ordinary church. It is not just for those who can understand the jargon and translate the theological language. It is a Covenant for the people and therefore should be built by the people.

The purpose of the Connect! Covenant

The purpose of the Connect! Covenant is to help provide some common ground to encourage Christians from around the world to have more confidence in working together. In order to encourage people to begin thinking through some of the issues in working together globally we want you to work with us to build the Covenant.

The Connect! Covenant will set out some key principles for partners to work through that will act as guidelines to their relationship. We would like you to be part of this process – here's how:

1. Think about experiences you have had in dealing with people from a different culture. What are the most important issues that need to be worked through to make sure such a relationship is well-founded and avoids misunderstandings?

2. Encourage your church leaders to think through the same questions and have their input to the Covenant from a local church perspective.

3. Contact other Christians you know – especially those in other parts of the world – and encourage them to have their say in developing the Connect! Covenant.

Your input to the Connect! Covenant

A website has been set up to give people from all over the world access to the process of developing the Connect! Covenant. Get on-line, have a look and have your say on what should be in the Covenant.

www.connect.nu

The Connect! Covenant is a means to an end. For many people their experience of working with people from different traditions or cultures has been one of misunderstandings, not unity. So often this division comes from wrong assumptions, incompatible and unrealistic expectations and poor communication. The Connect! Covenant is intended to provide some broad principles for people wanting to work together, helping to steer them around some of the pitfalls that can cause problems to arise. It will provide guidance on the issues to watch out for and hopefully enable partnerships between different groups to be more fruitful and rewarding. The Covenant provides a context in which difficult issues, such as differing expectations (especially in the area of money), can be discussed and agreed.

Contents of the Covenant

Here are some of the areas that the Connect! Covenant will cover:

Relationship
Successful partnerships are built on good relationships. Above everything else, mutual trust, understanding and confidence in each other's integrity have to be built. The development and preservation of a strong relationship has to be the principal commitment from both sides.

Communication
So often, a lack of communication or poor communication leads to difficulties in a relationship. The Connect! Covenant should include some commitment to a level and quality of communication between the partners.

Shared vision
Partnership should not be an end in itself – a sort of church-twinning. Rather, all concerned should share a vision of what the partnership should be for, and agree on what they believe can be achieved through it.

Compatibility
Denominational matters are not the issue here. Partnerships across or outside denominations can be rewarding and fruitful. For a partnership to work, however, there does need to be confidence on both sides that a basic compatibility exists in terms of an understanding of faith and a concern for outreach.

Expectations
People from very different backgrounds entering into some kind of relationship will inevitably have different expectations. Money issues can be particularly difficult. The Covenant should help people to be explicit about their expectations from the relationship and come to a point where expectations are fully understood and agreed.

Respect
There has to be mutual respect and a valuing of the partner's own culture for a partnership to thrive. A patronising or paternalistic attitude on one side will cause resentment on the other and sabotage prospects for developing a healthy partnership.

Interdependence
Every individual or group of people has something of value to learn and to share and must accept that the experience, understanding, values, preferences and culture of each party are equally valid and important. Each member of a partnership should seek to serve the other, and be willing to expose their own weaknesses to enable their partner to help them. The Connect! Covenant should ensure equality, mutuality and interdependence so that people actively seek out opportunities to receive as well as give.

Sharing of power
Greater access to technology and material goods can often tempt a western partner to assume the dominant role in a partnership and impose their own goals and priorities on it. Explicit efforts should be made to guard against this and to ensure partners feel empowered to set their own priorities and relate on a basis of equality.

Reliability
Healthy meaningful partnerships can only develop when each side knows the other can be relied on to keep their word.

Finance
As they grow, many relationships develop a financial dimension. Unfortunately it is in this area that relationships can often come unstuck. It is important therefore to

make sure that finance is specifically covered in a covenant relationship, in terms of both expectations and the practical issues of how decisions will be made and accountability assured.

The above areas are ones that we believe need to be considered as part of the Connect! Covenant. Which of them do you think are the most important? Are there others that we've missed? Go on-line at www.connect.nu and tell us what you think.

Summary

❏ The Connect! Covenant is being developed to provide guidelines to help the church across the world work more effectively together.

❏ The Covenant will be developed by ordinary Christians from around the world via the Internet.

❏ Have your say at www.connect.nu

Questions for discussion

1. What do you think about the appropriateness of each area of the Covenant as outlined above? Which of these do you see as most important?

2. Are there areas not included above which you think should be part of the Connect! Covenant? What are these missing areas?

8

Spice it up!

This book aims to give you a vision for mission in a globalised, postmodern world, and to encourage you to try new ways of doing it. But what options are there for doing things differently? In many walks of life, it seems that the barriers to actually changing are not a lack of belief in the new, but a lack of imagination or concrete ideas. The issue therefore is often not 'Why?' or 'What?' but 'How?' The purpose of this chapter is to introduce you to a few ideas that might begin to get your imagination working and open the door to doing some new things in global mission. For this reason little space is devoted here to traditional ways of supporting mission, like giving to mission agencies and to missionaries, praying, communicating, and welcoming back missionaries to the UK. These have been the staples of mission-minded churches for many years and will probably continue to attract a major portion of missionary giving from many churches for years to come.

This chapter is about less traditional ways of doing mission. Though not necessarily new, they could add a new dimension to your church life and mission interest.

Take your partners

Partnership seems to have become an overused term but an underused reality. We would all sign up to the principle of working together with others to get things done, but how many genuine partnerships are you a part of? Partnership is an incredibly important concept in mission and one that we need to explore and develop as the global church begins to flex its muscles and work more as a global network.

Partnership has become part of the vocabulary within mission circles. Agencies talk about their partners in another country, usually meaning a local church or another mission organisation. 'Missionary' is now a little-used term, with many organisations labelling the people that work cross-culturally as 'Mission Partners'. Within global mission therefore, partnerships can be of many kinds: individual to church, church to agency, agency to agency, church to project, etc.

All of these are valid and worthwhile and the more that different people and groups within the global church work together, the greater the achievements our efforts are likely to produce. One growing form of partnership, and the one we want to focus on here is church-to-church partnering. This is not a new model in mission, but is one that seems to be on the rise and that fits very well within our globalised, postmodern world. It is also one that we are likely to be seeing far more of in the coming years.

Daniel Rickett, Director of Partner Development for Partners International, the American Mission Agency, defines a complementary partnership as 'a relationship between ministries and people who share common aspirations, strive to achieve them together, and do so in a spirit of cooperation and brotherly love. By

> this definition, partnership involves making the part-
> ner an extension of your own ministry.'[1]

Setting up a partnership with a church in another country is often not easy because of the differences there may be between you – geographical, cultural, language, economic. But churches that have persevered, worked through the issues and established a genuine partnership have almost invariably found that they have gained far more than they have given. Experience shows that a good cross-cultural partnership is likely to: enrich your church life, broaden your understanding of the global church, get your church members directly involved in mission, and profoundly affect the outlook and values of those who get actively involved. If you are looking for changes within your own church, partnering a church in another country is a sure-fire way to stir things up!

Getting a church partnership going

For most churches, partnerships grow out of existing relationships. You may have someone from your church working with a church in another part of the world and can begin to build a relationship with that church that goes beyond just sending one person. What connections do you currently have that may be the seeds of a new partnership?

Listed below are some of the things you will need to think through to begin getting a partnership going:
- Is this something that could inspire and involve large numbers of people within the church? How can you get

---

[1]   Daniel Rickett, *Making your Partnership Work* (Enumclaw, WA: Winepress Publishing, 2002), p.23.

broad ownership of the partnership and particularly the commitment of your church leadership?

● What are your aims for the partnership – both what you hope to receive as well as to give? You may want to lend or receive support in mission outreach and church planting, give training or aid, do relief work, or any combination of these. Consider if you could benefit from receiving mission workers into your community from another country.

Christian Life Church, Hereford, with about 150 members, has had a relationship with the missionary movement Go to the Nations since about 1995. They have received several Brazilian couples into their church for a year or two at a time, and sent members of their own congregation to Brazilian churches. The relationship has had a profound effect on the Hereford church. In the words of David Marshall their pastor, it has 'opened our eyes to the need and call of missions ... More and more people in our congregation are realising that there is a part for them to play ... The key to this is the understanding that we, *as a body* are called to missions. Some go, some serve those going, some give and some pray. It has quite changed the dynamics of the church here.'

The Brazilians have also had a dramatic effect on the wider Christian community in Hereford, playing an influential role in bringing about a remarkable degree of unity and joint action between the different churches and denominations.

● Is there a particular church, country or area that you would like to partner with?

Christ Church, Fulwood (with around 1,000 Sunday attenders), has two partnerships, one with a church in the Ukraine and another with a church in Romania, both of which started in the early 1990s after the fall of Communism. Christ Church's aim in both countries was to encourage and strengthen the local churches' evangelistic efforts, and in Romania they have also supplied relief aid. They also wanted to train some of Christ Church's members in evangelism and encourage enthusiasm for mission. Christ Church's objectives are being met in both partnerships, and they feel they have been greatly enriched by the relationships and by the opportunities for service and witness which the partnerships have provided.

- Do you have trusted people in your church willing to become 'champions' for the partnership, putting time and energy into getting it going and maintaining it once it's underway?

St Mary's and St Paul's Churches (C of E) *in Thornbury, Gloucestershire* established a link with a parish in Uganda, but the relationship really took off once a recently retired couple in the congregation took a lead in visiting the Ugandan parish, publicising the link in Thornbury, and fundraising.

- Are there trusted contacts at the other end? At least one person may be enough to start with, but it would be better if this could be broadened out to include others, especially if money enters the relationship. It is difficult to exaggerate the importance of building your partnership on a good relationship with people you can trust, and who understand the need for regular, open communication to keep the partnership going. You may already have such a relationship on which a partnership could be built.

> *Altrincham Baptist Church's* partnership with Jinja, Uganda, arose from friendships between members of their congregation and members of a Ugandan Christian Dance Company that had visited the UK several times in the 1990s.

● Depending on what you want to achieve, decide whether it would be better for your partner to be a church, a specific project or an agency. Find out about power relationships in the church culture or denomination in the country where you are thinking of partnering. Be aware that in some cultures and/or some denominations the structural relationships may leave local churches with little autonomy to undertake initiatives of this kind.

> *Emmanuel Church, Wimbledon,* wanted to establish a partnership to support evangelism in India. They decided the most effective way of doing this was to partner with an indigenous Indian mission agency.

● Finally, and most importantly, do you have a sense that God is calling your church to this? Is it just a fascinating idea that attracts your interest, or do you feel a God-inspired pull to explore this further? Time to get the knee-pads out!

Just as there can be enormous benefits from entering into a partnership, there are also lots of potential pitfalls to avoid. The following 'dos and don'ts' will help you build a healthy and productive relationship.

Do

1. *Build genuine relationships* involving a number of people on both sides, before moving into a partnership. You must be sure that you can trust the people you are thinking of partnering with, and that there is sufficient understanding, sympathy and compatibility between you to be able to bridge cultural and/or denominational differences. Building genuine relationships that will last, takes time!

2. *Make your intentions clear and build a shared vision* when you move towards partnership.

3. *Make sure that the people at the other end understand the need for regular two-way communication* and will actually provide the flow of information that will enable you to maintain interest and support at your end. Without it partnerships die.

4. *Find out about the culture* of the country in which you are partnering.

5. *Take advice* from those who know the country and the culture – possibly a mission agency.

6. *Make every effort to understand* the interests and concerns of the church in the other country, both nationally and locally.

7. *Use the Connect! Covenant* to establish a basis of mutual understanding and shared values on which your partnership can be founded.

8. *Be willing to receive as well as to give.*

9. *When you are ready to move from relationship-building to partnering for specific purposes, agree on shared goals for the partnership.* We recommend you do this in writing if that fits with the partner's culture. Otherwise an oral agreement that you could confirm in writing would do.

10. *Ensure that mutual accountability and transparency* are built into the relationship from the start.

11. *Be prepared to make mistakes* and to get hurt. Partnering can be a messy business, which is why it has to be founded on strong relationships.

> Ajitha Fernando, National Director of Youth for Christ in Sri Lanka, wrote: 'By and large, I think Western people get deceived very easily … Very often, those who impress a Westerner are people that our people are very suspicious of. Sometimes [Westerners] end up feeling that you can't trust an Asian … The problem is that they trusted the wrong person … It could be that these people can speak well and are good in English – the motivator type. They can present their programme in a very exciting way. Generally, I think this country [the USA] looks very much for people who are motivated … Motivation has to be verbally expressed. If it's not, they may feel that someone is not really motivated.'[2]

---

2   Daniel Rickett, 'Seven Mistakes Partners Make and How to Avoid Them', *Evangelical Missions Quarterly*, July 2001, pp.312-13.

Don't

1. *Commit too early* to a partnership. Build relationships and grow in understanding first.

2. *Rush to offer money.* Some agencies advise against any transfer of money at all because of the likelihood that it will create a fatal imbalance in the relationship. Others would say that the economic gap between the northern and southern hemispheres is so huge, and the poverty in a partnering community often so dire, that it would be inconceivable not to try to help. But if you do feel you should give, it is advisable to wait before committing funds, and then be discerning in what you give to. Above all try to avoid creating an unequal relationship or inappropriate dependency. See Chapter 10 for further advice on money matters.

3. *Try to dominate or control the relationship*, even if you are giving money.

4. *Restrict yourselves to partnering within your church tradition or denomination.* If there are trusting relationships, shared convictions and common values and priorities in ministry, these are more important than keeping within a denomination. In fact partnering within a denomination creates its own problems. Other churches from the same denomination in the poorer country can feel jealous at the attention and (often) material benefits that a local partnering church is receiving. Denominational leaders in that church's area can also be suspicious or jealous.

> 'Partnerships are built on trust. Without it, they simply won't work.'[3]

---

[3] Rickett, Making Your Partnership Work, p.75.

You may decide that your church is not currently at a place where you are ready for a full-blown partnership with another church, but you can see the benefits of having a strong and active link with Christians working in another part of the world. A good alternative may be to partner with a specific project that is being organised by a mission agency. You may find that you can get many of the benefits of direct contact and ongoing relationship, etc. without some of the uncertainties that can crop up. Having a trusted intermediary to help you broker the relationship and provide some greater feeling of security and account-ability may be the right next step. Many mission agencies like Oasis now have schemes that will enable you to part-ner with a specific project – ask around.

Further resources on partnering

www.connect.nu/partner

Go to the above Connect! website and look for helpful links to organisations who can help you with setting up a partnership.

Radstock Ministries exists to help local churches become directly involved in mission. They help UK churches to set up partnerships with churches in eastern Europe.

> Radstock Ministries
> 2a Argyle Street
> Mexborough
> South Yorkshire
> S64 9BW
> Tel: 01709 582345
> Website: www.radstock.org
> Email: info@radstock.org

Partnership in World Mission, an Anglican body, produces useful guidelines on parish-to-parish links that contain a fund of practical advice based on years of experience. These are available on the PWM website. Despite the Anglican context much of the content will be relevant to non-Anglican congregations wishing to partner cross-culturally.

Website: www.pwm-web.org.uk

Daniel Rickett, *Making your Partnership Work* (Enumclaw, WA: Winepress Publishing, 2002). This book is intended primarily for agencies partnering with each other and it may therefore be unduly prescriptive and managerial in approach for churches seeking to partner. But it contains a fund of advice based on long experience that is highly relevant.

Church to Church Links, available from Enquiry and Marketing, CMS, Partnership House, 157 Waterloo Road, London SE1 8UU. Tel: 020 7928 8681. Price £3.50. This is a guide intended for Anglican churches seeking to set up a church link, but much of its advice will also be relevant to those of other denominations or none.

Business as mission

A meeting of over 400 African church leaders in March 2001 declared that the need to empower the poor was the primary need of the church in Africa.

As people's understanding of mission enlarges, so too does their understanding of who can be involved. Many mission agencies now recognise that Christian businesspeople working in other parts of the world are being used by God to have a significant influence on the societies and people around them. Many churches however, have been slow to value the businesspeople in their congregation (apart from what they can donate to the church) and few seem positively to encourage such members to see themselves as part of God's global mission force.

The Transformational Business Network has been set up to link Christians wanting to do mission through business, enabling them to share experience and resources. At a meeting arranged by the Network in London in June 2002, the businesspeople present said they attached high priority to the need for training of church pastors to enable them to support members of their congregation doing business as mission.

People with business skills can get involved in mission in several different ways. Some of these may be about an individual's lifestyle and witness as they travel. Even for those who seldom travel overseas there are ways in which business skills can be used to help members of a community or church in another country to earn a living.

Why not invite some businesspeople in your congregation to a gathering and get them started on thinking about business as mission, and what they could do? And think too about how your congregation could support and value them if they decide to get actively involved. Here are a few ideas.

1. *Using business skills and travel opportunities for mission*
   Businesspeople who travel to other countries, especially where the church is weak or persecuted, might be able to make contact with and encourage local

Christians. Or if self-employed they could give their services free for a portion of their working week, to help a mission, aid agency or local church.

Tony Cherrington runs his own computer support business in Rochester, Kent.

He donates his skills and some of his time to Cyberark, a project of the Vines Centre Trust that distributes donated computer equipment to individuals and organisations in the UK and to educational institutions and programmes in eastern Europe, India and elsewhere.

---

2. *Mentoring and discipling emerging entrepreneurs in needy areas*
   Groups of businesspeople are already visiting areas of central Asia, Africa and elsewhere to train and encourage Christians from those areas in business skills. More details are available from the Transformational Business Network.

3. *Setting up a business in a needy country*
   In many countries in eastern Europe people able to set up and run commercial businesses are in desperately short supply. While the bureaucracy and other factors can be deterrents, the difference that a business run along Christian lines can make to the local economy, and its witness to how Christian values can be reflected in the conduct of business, can be considerable.

In 2000 Norman Fraser from the UK and three Moldovan partners set up Brains Direct, an IT Software outsourcing company which employs around fifty Moldovan staff. The company has normal business objectives, but it is having a transformational effect on society in Moldova, a former Soviet Republic with 4 million inhabitants and the poorest country in Europe.

Brains Direct observes good employment practices, has world-class corporate clients, and works with the Moldovan universities to ensure training of students is geared to business needs. The directors also work with the Moldovan Government (which is desperate to attract businesses to Moldova) to ensure that they do not create a regulatory environment likely to deter businesses from considering operating in Moldova.

4. *Helping small businesses in another country to start or expand by providing capital, advice and training*
This is a great way of helping people in areas of acute poverty or unemployment to get a living and maintain their dignity. Many aid agencies are heavily involved in this kind of development work and churches can get directly involved too, especially if they already have a trusted partner church or agency in a particular country.

The City Church, Worcester, has about 150 members. In the mid-1990s they had built a relationship with a Baptist church in the Ukraine, where unemployment was a huge problem. With guidance from business-people in their congregation City Church set up a fund of $5,000 (increased to $11,000 a year later) and appointed three Ukrainian fund managers, who were trusted and capable members of that church, to manage the fund within a framework set up by City

▶

Church. Hard currency loans were offered to local Ukrainians who could present sensible business proposals. Members of City Church audit the fund records and speak to loan recipients every six months or so.

Between 1999 and mid-2002, 26 loans of between $300 and $3,000 were made to 11 small businesses (such as a roadside kiosk). Five new businesses were established employing 6 people, 2 existing businesses were able to grow and employ 11 people between them, and 4 profitable one-off transactions were made. None of those who borrowed from the fund defaulted on their loan. City Church has now increased the fund which is making loans of greater value available.

Further resources on business as mission

www.connect.nu/business

Global Connections has a Business Associates Scheme for Christians whose business or professional lives include some degree of international involvement. Their website includes some useful papers, briefings and web links.

Website: www.globalconnections.co.uk/business.asp

The Transformational Business Network website can only be entered by members, but you can look at the first page and then ask to sign up. The website link is: http://uk.groups.yahoo.com/group/TBNetwork/

Enquiries about the Network can also be emailed to: bam@oval.com

Take up a cause

The Jubilee 2000 debt campaign provided a fantastic example of how mass mobilisation of ordinary people (mostly Christian) can influence big issues. Our world is full of many injustices and globalisation seems to be adding fuel to the fire. As Christians we have a clear call to stand against injustice and oppression and yet many of us do very little to make a difference.

God calls us to be involved in the world around us – down the street and in the global arena. Taking up a particular cause, as a church, and campaigning for change is part of our calling as global Christians. There are many issues to choose from: world poverty, the environment, trade justice, the spread of AIDS – the list seems endless. The key is to find something that a number of people within your church are concerned about and find ways of bringing the issue alive. There are things that we can do to have an influence and the more people that get involved, the better.

> 'The foundations of the kingdom of God were laid in the lives of the poor ... Jesus looked at the world not through the eyes of a king but through the eyes of the poor ... Jesus suggests that, even if it may surprise some, the poor are of greater importance in his kingdom than those in high positions (Luke 14) ... The Church ... must always put the role of the poor first within the Church.'[4]

---

[4] Eddie Bruwer, *Beggars Can be Choosers*, (Institute for Missiological and Ecumenical Research, University of Pretoria, 2001), p.60.

There are plenty of organisations, both Christian and secular, that aim to raise awareness of issues and facilitate ways for people to have a voice on them. Ways of campaigning for a cause can include:

- writing letters to foreign embassies or to companies to express your concerns;
- collecting signatures for petitions to be sent to companies, embassies or government departments;
- writing to or meeting your MP to ask them to raise a matter with the appropriate UK government department;
- joining marches or protests;
- collecting money for relief to be sent to areas that have suffered a disaster.

Don't forget the persecuted church. There are 74 countries around the world where Christians are persecuted for their faith, and in many of these Christians are already on the margins of society. Their fate is given little coverage in the secular western press, but prayer and practical support from western Christians can make a huge difference to them.

What would you like to take issue with?

Further help on taking up a cause

www.connect.nu/causes

The Connect! website has links to a number of organisations who can help you get informed about and actively involved in an issue of concern to you.

The following are just a selection from the many agencies that aim to address the concerns mentioned.

Tearfund: An evangelical Christian agency that provides developmental and relief aid to poor communities around the world.

Tearfund
100 Church Road,
Teddington
Middlesex TW11 8QE
Tel: 0845 355 8355
Website: www.tearfund.org
Email: enquiry@tearfund.org

The Barnabas Fund provides news and prayer requests on persecuted Christians, and channels funds to those most in need of help.

The Barnabas Fund
The Old Rectory
River Street
Pewsey
Wiltshire SN9 5DB
Tel: 01672 564938
Website: www.barnabasfund.org
Email: info@barnabasfund.org

Open Doors International exists to serve the persecuted church worldwide. The head office is in the USA but there are offices in several other countries including the UK.

Open Doors International
PO Box 6
Witney
Oxon OX29 6WG
Tel: 01993 885400
Website: www.gospelcom.net/od/
Email: helpdesk@opendoorsuk.org

Friends of the Earth is a secular organisation that campaigns on environmental issues worldwide.

>Friends of the Earth
>26-28 Underwood Street
>London N1 7JQ.
>Tel: 020 7490 1555
>Website: www.foe.co.uk
>Email: info@foe.co.uk

The Christian NGO Advocacy Forum (CNAF) website is a networking and information resource for the advocacy work of Christian development NGOs, human rights and mission organisations.

Website: www.cnaf.org.uk
Email: info@cnaf.org.uk

Adopt an unreached people group

A 'people' in this context is an ethnic group, a collection of individuals who are bound together by a common cultural heritage and language, but are not necessarily confined by geographical or political borders. One nation state may contain many people groups. An 'unreached people' will have had little or no opportunity to hear the gospel of Jesus Christ.

A number of mission agencies encourage churches to 'adopt' an unreached people group somewhere in the world. The primary purpose is to encourage prayer and interest in the people group. Some agencies will arrange for members of supporting churches to visit 'their' unreached people group.

Bournemouth Family Church (BFC) had built up close links with a group of pastors in Uganda and wanted to adopt an unreached people group in a nearby country. Wycliffe Bible Translators put them in touch with the only Christian from a suitable people group. Two members of BFC visited this contact in Kenya and were used by God to heal him miraculously of hepatitis! The contact later spent three months at BFC building up good relationships, resulting in strong support across the congregation for the work amongst this people. There are now plans afoot for members of BFC to cooperate with the Ugandan churches and Wycliffe in evangelism and church-planting amongst this people group.

Practical steps to adopting an unreached people group

There is no prescribed way of doing this, but Interlinks at Global Connections have produced a useful advisory booklet, 'Adopt a People', that can be obtained from them free of charge. Briefly, and with their permission to draw on that booklet, some sensible early steps would be:

1. *Pray* – for guidance to start with, and right through the process.

2. *Consult widely* within the congregation and especially the leadership.

3. *Choose a people group* – maybe one you already have an interest in, or mission connection with. Or one in an area of the world you'd like to know more about.

4. *Approach a mission agency* if you know one that is working in the area you have chosen. Otherwise approach

Interlinks who can tell you what agencies have a focus on that area. Some may already have an 'Adopt-a-People' programme.

5. *Appoint a coordinator* within your congregation for all the activities to do with your adopted people.

6. *Research* the adopted people using the mission agency, the Internet, etc, and publicise what you learn within the congregation.

7. *Launch the 'Adoption'*, e.g. with a special service.

Further help on adopting an unreached people group

Interlinks at Global Connections can supply the booklet 'Adopt a People' and help put you in touch with suitable mission agencies. Contact:

> Interlinks @ Global Connections
> Whitefield House
> 186 Kennington Park Road
> London SE11 4BT
> Tel: 020 7207 2156
> Website: www.globalconnections.co.uk/inter-links.asp
> Email: interlinks@globalconnections.co.uk

Take off!

Go! Go! Go! ... to see for yourself what it is like to be poor and marginalised in India, Africa, south east Asia or anywhere else in the Two-Thirds World. And to see too what a difference Christians can make in such circumstances. If possible, lend a hand yourself.

If your church is already linked to someone working in mission in such a country then there's a lot to be gained from going to see them. You can help strengthen links between your missionary and their church, give them encouragement, and bring back firsthand news to the church.

Emmanuel Church, South Croydon, encourages visits by its members to those whom they support in mission overseas. 'The more people we can get to see mission at the coal face, the keener they will be for the rest of their lives to promote such work.' They discovered some years ago that the best mission investment they could make was to send their clergy on such trips. Those who go return brimming with enthusiasm for mission and eager to share it with the wider congregation. And their mission partners get great encouragement from such visits.

If your church has or wants a partnership with a church in another country, visits are indispensable for ensuring that real relationships are built and maintained.

If you don't have a current link with any particular country but want to learn more at first hand about mission work and living in the Two-Thirds World, some agencies will arrange short visits to a wide range of countries, and may give you a chance to 'get your hands dirty'.

Christian Vocations produce the *Short-Term Service Directory*. It lists a huge number of organisations that offer short-term opportunities all over the world and gives contact information for each of them. What about getting a copy for your church office and making it available to people looking for opportunities to get involved?

It is common for young people to take a 'year out for God' and many agencies can arrange this. But you don't have to be under 30 to go on short- or medium-term service. Mature individuals with skills also have much to offer.

> A woman with four grown-up children gave up her teaching job in the UK to work with Oasis India teaching tailoring to women from city slums.

Further resources on short-term mission visits

CMS. An Anglican Mission Agency which welcomes those of other Christian backgrounds or denominations. Has a number of programmes for short- and longer-term mission experience including some for young people, and Praxis, which offers two or three week visits for those aged 25+.

> CMS
> Partnership House
> 157 Waterloo Road
> London SE1 8AX
> Tel: 020 7928 8681
> Website: www.cms-uk.org

The Oasis Trust offers a whole range of 'Global Opportunities' for individuals and groups. They seek to find the most suitable placement to meet the requirements of each individual, whether it's gap years, summer mission teams, or short-, medium- and long-term professional placements with its partners in other countries.

> The Oasis Trust – Global Action
> 115 Southwark Bridge Road
> London SE1 0AX

Tel: 020 7 450 9000
Website: www.oasistrust.org/go

Christian Vocations. An organisation dedicated to providing good advice and options for all kinds of Christian service, Christian Vocations produces the Short-term Service Directory every year. This handbook contains information about dozens of short-term mission programmes run by UK mission agencies and others.

Christian Vocations
St James House
Trinity Road
Dudley DY1 1JB
Tel: 01384 233511
Website: www.christianvocations.org
Email: info@christianvocations.org

Keep it going!

Once you have got the mission strategy and range of mission activities that seem right for your church, the big issue is how to maintain momentum and keep the congregation interested and motivated. Try some of these ideas, which have been tried and tested by other churches:

● Make mission a regular and interesting part of your main Sunday services. Live phone or video links with 'your' missionaries or those on short-term assignments can have a big impact on the congregation. Regular mission spots, and mention of those on mission work, will help press home the message that mission is an integral part of your church's life.

- Encourage home groups each to 'adopt' someone in mission who is linked to your church. The home group can take or share responsibility for praying for them, welcoming them home, and representing them within the church as required.

- Regular articles with a mission focus in the church magazine.

- Outward visits by members of the congregation and pastors to places with which your church has some mission link.

- Inward visits from a partner church or from one of 'your' missionaries.

- Hand over the whole service – or as much of it as they want – to those that you support in mission when they come home. This will give them freedom to tell their story as they want.

- Encourage short-term mission trips by both young and mature people, especially to places in which you already have a mission interest.

- Hold annual mission Fun Days or Activity Days, with a range of activities and stalls to interest all the family while also publicising the mission work that you support. All proceeds to go to mission work.

Summary

Why not try doing mission differently by:

❏ Starting a church-to-church partnership

❏ Encouraging businesspeople in your church to see the potential of business as mission

▶

❏ Becoming advocates for the global poor, trade justice, the persecuted church, or other good causes

❏ Adopting an unreached people

❏ Making short mission-oriented trips as part of your church's mission activities

Be sure to develop a strategy for how to maintain enthusiasm for mission in your church.

Questions for discussion

1. Would your church benefit from trying some of the less traditional mission activities proposed in this chapter? If so, which one(s) seem most suitable?

2. How do you think this type of mission activity would:

   ● benefit your church

   ● draw on the skills and abilities of the members, and/or

   ● enable it to give to others?

3. How could you put this idea to your church leadership/mission committee?

4. Do you think your church should be more involved with global issues such as trade justice, poverty, the environment, or the persecuted church? If so, what can you do about it?

5. Which of the ideas for maintaining a congregation's mission enthusiasm would work in your church? How could you encourage the church to adopt them?

Further help on maintaining mission interest and involvement

Joy Piper, *Bringing the World to Your Church* (N.p.: WEC Publications, 2000) – a lively, practical and up-to-date book full of ideas on how to encourage global mission involvement and enthusiasm in local churches.

Stephen Gaukroger, *Why Bother with Mission?* (Leicester: InterVarsity Press, 1996) – a useful book aimed at ordinary Christians, with a particularly good chapter on 'A Mission Minded Church'.

9

Where do we Start?

Developing a mission strategy

Hopefully by now you have seen the possibilities and responsibilities of every church to be involved in global mission. It is possible, it can work and *you* can do it! The next question is 'How?' 'How can we as a church get involved?' 'Ultimately what involvement would best suit us and what steps can we begin to take to get from where we are now to where we would like to be?'

The real message is 'get deliberate'. For most churches the involvement they have had in global mission in the past has rarely been part of an organised, thought-out strategy. Support has been

St Barnabas, Kensington (Anglican) has a membership of 300–350. At least 10 per cent of its church budget is given to mission, plus the proceeds of an annual mission gift day. The bulk of its mission funding goes to groups and individuals with which it or its members have direct links. The church aims to strike a balance in its funding support between practical ministries and preaching-teaching-based ones.

given to a denominational agency. People may have gone from the church to serve with a mission society and reappeared every few years for something called a 'furlough'. Young people have gone off on gap years or summer mission teams. Many of these existing activities and relationships may be very healthy and positive for all involved, others may be hangovers from the past that have little relevance to the church today.

In any field of life it is a healthy thing occasionally to take time to stand back and review the state of play. It can be very helpful to put ourselves under a microscope and ask probing questions: 'Why do we do that?' 'Is this still relevant?' 'What do we want to achieve/What is our goal?' In the light of the incredible changes taking place in our world and particularly in global mission, is it time for your church to evaluate its attitude to and involvement in the global mission of the church?

Strategy – being deliberate

Some people get put off at the thought of developing a strategy – it sounds too business-like and organised and leaves no space for spontaneity and the organic development of letting things move at their own pace. In fact, developing a strategy is all about being deliberate about achieving something. It makes us focus first on what it is that we want to achieve, helping to prevent us from simply going round in circles and never being effective in our efforts. Our strategy then helps us set a course to get from where we are to where we want to be. It need not be a rigid thing that acts like a straightjacket but can allow us to evaluate opportunities that come up to see if they are actually going to get us closer to where we want to be.

Some churches have developed a clear statement of vision and goals and a strategy to achieve these. Some of these have aspects covering their involvement in the world or guidelines to focus their thinking and support for mission. For years, world mission in many churches has been seen as a bit of a minority interest – something that the mission committee tinker with at the periphery of the church and something that is done by others, 'in the mission field'. Bryan Knell, in his booklet 'Encouraging World Mission', strongly advises against preparing a 'world mission strategy' for a local church. Instead he advocates preparing a 'strategy for the church that involves the world'. In a globalised world where geography and distance are increasingly irrelevant, this is good advice. If your church strategy doesn't take into account 'the ends of the earth' as well as 'Judea' and 'Samaria', then maybe some revision is required!

Stopsley Baptist Church, with about 360 members, gives about 10 per cent of the church's budget to mission, but much additional funding is given as personal gifts to projects and individuals. The church's big vision for mission is 'striving to become a globally-focused, mission-sending church'. Its strategy is based around the people it sends, so for the years 2003–2005 it encompasses south Asia, east Asia, Africa and the Balkans. Its mission statement includes some specific goals, e.g. 'to send out five long-term missionaries by September 2002'. This was achieved, and they have set the same goal for the next three years – i.e. five more missionaries.

Structurally, Stopsley Baptist distinguishes between mission within the UK on the one hand, and outside it on the other, but although this has administrative advantages the church is contemplating abolishing the distinction because they think it is detrimental to a healthy view of mission.

Gold Hill Baptist Church, with 600–700 members, spends 25 per cent of its budget on cross-cultural mission. It has two key criteria for deciding what ministries to support:

1. They must aim at unreached people groups.

2. They must be one of the most effective ways of reaching those people.

All the missionaries they support (about twenty in all) are church members, and almost all their funding follows their people. The church aims to train future missionaries and support and pastor those who are sent out. If members of the congregation wanted to work in ministries that did not fit their criteria the church would not formally support them, although it would bless them and want the best for them.

Whether you have a church strategy or not, it makes sense to take stock of where your church sits on the issue of global mission and begin to dream a little as to where you would like it to go. There are no right or wrong answers. If mission is already thriving in your church across all ages and your existing approach seems to be working well, that's great. (Actually we'd love to hear from you, learn from you and help others learn from your experience.) But if you are starting from near scratch or are dissatisfied with your current approach to global mission and contemplating a drastic overhaul, we recommend that you take a strategic approach to help you move forward.

How to develop a strategy for global mission

There are many ways to go about developing a strategy and you may have within your church the skills to develop and implement your own process. The remainder of this chapter is designed as an aid to give some ideas of how you might take this forward. Pick bits out, add to it, completely redo it. It is offered as a place to start to help you develop something that is relevant and useful for your situation.

In order to actually interest the people in your church and get them involved, it is important that your strategy starts with who they are, the community around them and uses their interests in the world as the jumping off point. In churches where global mission is flourishing it is almost always a result of congregational interest and involvement because the mission agenda is scratching where people itch. If your church is a majority black Afro-Caribbean church, a mission strategy of supporting work amongst Muslims in Pakistan is probably not the most obvious place to start! (Although it might be a great broadening experience further down the road.)

A word about process

One of the aims of developing a new mission strategy has to be to get widespread ownership and involvement in global mission across the church. While much of the work may be done by a small group, it is important that your minister and church leaders are seen to support and participate in the process. And the more that the whole church is involved in developing the strategy, the greater the ownership will be. Find ways of allowing as many people as possible to input to the process. Well-designed questionnaires can be a very

good way of collecting a lot of information from a
wide range of people. Special home group sessions
that produce specific feedback can also be helpful.
Seek to get all parts of the church engaged in the
process – not just the vocal ones.

There are many ways to develop a strategy – from the top-
down vision-led strategy developed by a small group of
leaders to the bottom-up, democratic strategy developed
by widespread consultation. Whichever place on the spectrum best suits your church, it helps to follow a logical
process that will help you to come up with a strategy
appropriate to your circumstances. The following steps
may help guide you towards a logical process:

Step 1. Who are we?

> Building up a picture of the church family – age
> profile, ethnic background, employment patterns,
> etc. and also of the community around the church.

*Step 2. What international interests do people in our church
have?*

> Many people within the church will already have
> interests in other parts of the world or certain
> global issues. Try to get a fuller picture of what
> these interests are to help you see if there are any
> significant themes that already exist.

Step 3. What experience of global mission have we had?

> Are there people in the church who have experience
> of global mission? What are the foundations in global
> mission that we already have that we might build on?

Step 4. How much is global mission part of our church life?

> Evaluate the current level of interest in the church in global mission. What are some of the indicators that point to an interest or lack of it within the way the church operates and organises itself?

Step 5. What forms of mission would our congregation like to get involved with?

> Find out what your church members would actually like to do, or support, in global mission. And find out who is prepared to be actively involved.

Step 6. Building blocks for a new strategy

> Taking all the above into consideration, what should be the core themes of our mission strategy that will reflect and build on who we are, our interests and what experience we have of the world?

The core purpose here is to develop a strategy that will get people within the church interested and involved because it starts where they are. That's why so much emphasis is placed on first evaluating your situation. If a church's involvement in global mission is to be owned by a large proportion of the church, it has to interest and excite them. It's worth taking the time therefore to find out what interests people and using this as the starting point for a strategy.

The place of prayer

In some ways it goes without saying, but make sure that the whole process of thinking about global mission in your church is surrounded by prayer. Ask God to give you direction and discernment as you seek a

▶ new way forward and also for the creativity and openness to take on new things. A managed process of developing strategy does not exclude seeking God's guidance – the two need to work together.

Copies of questionnaires that may be of use in developing a strategy can be found at www.connect.nu / strategy.

Constructing your mission strategy

Hopefully at this point you'll have a good idea about some of the elements of your new strategy. This stage of actually putting a strategy together is key as you make all sorts of judgements about which avenues to pursue and which to leave aside. There is no blueprint for this but to help you think through what areas your strategy might cover have a look at the list below and use this to help structure your thoughts.

Vision

● Is there some overarching, big-picture goal that summarises and focuses our intentions?

PROCESS TIP

Process here is critical. The more people who can be included in the decision-making, the better. You may want to present a number of options and get everyone in the church to rank them with their order of preference or vote on them in some other way. If you do this with different groups – particularly with younger people as a separate group – you may find that different parts of the church are more drawn to one thing than another.

Sending and supporting

- What is going to be our strategy towards supporting people who feel called to work overseas?
- Will we only support people who are working in places, with agencies or on particular projects that are part of our strategic focus?
- If members of our church are applying to work with a mission agency, how involved do we as a church want to be in their selection process, in decisions concerning their placement and in their ongoing pastoral care once they have gone?

Geography

- Is there some area of the world, particular country or people group that we want to focus on?

> **TWINNING**
>
> These days, many towns and boroughs have started twinning links with particular places in another part of the world. The same is true of many Anglican dioceses through their 'Companion Links'. If you have no obvious geographical focus but feel that one would be helpful, it may be worth doing a little research within your denomination and/or locality to see if there are some options through existing twinning arrangments. The Local Government International Bureau promotes such links and can supply details of links that already exist. Contact them at LGIB, Local Government House, London, SW1P 3HZ. Tel: 020 7664 3100. Email: enquiries@lgib.gov.uk

Relationships with organisations

- Are there particular mission agencies that we have had a good relationship with and would like to work closely with in the future?

- Are there other agencies that we have heard about that might be able to help us implement our strategy?

Type of work

- Are we particularly interested in education, healthcare, church planting, street kids, AIDS orphans, emergency relief or some other type of work or group of people?

Issue

- Is there some global issue that particularly interests us and that we are keen to get more involved in (e.g. debt, the environment, fair trade)?

Receiving

- Are there particular things that we as church lack and can see the possibility of receiving from Christians in another part of the world?

- Are there things happening in the church in other parts of the world that interest us and from which we would like to learn?

- How can we learn and receive from the global church?

Finance

- How are we going to finance our involvement in global mission?

● Will we set aside a proportion of our annual church budget, ask individuals to give specifically for global mission and/or for their preferred projects as part of their covenanted giving, or have additional collections or gift days specifically focused on global mission? Or all of these?

Organisation and people

● Do we have people in the congregation who are able and willing to devote time to developing and maintaining our global mission interests?

● What sort of structures should we have to champion our interest in global mission? Should we establish a 'Global Issues Team' or some other group?

● Are we going to keep our involvement in local and national mission activities separate from our global ones and have two (or three) different structures, or should we combine them in some way?

Evaluating a strategy that includes a partnership

● If in the process of constructing your strategy you decide that you'd like to set up a partnership with a church or agency in another country, you may find it helpful to use the Connect! Covenant as a benchmark. The Connect! Covenant is intended to provide some guidelines for people wishing to work together across different cultures. As Chapter 7 explains, the Covenant will be finalised in the light of input to the website www.connect.nu from around the world, and the final version will be available during 2004 and displayed on the website. But if you are reading this before then, look again at what chapter 7 says about the areas the Covenant is likely to cover.

● Whilst you're developing ideas for a partnership, keep the principles of the Covenant in mind and monitor your ideas against it. As you develop the strategy keep asking how you can implement and live up to the standards it sets out.

Some words of caution

Horses for courses

There is no single right answer. There is no one 'off the peg' global mission strategy for a church. You can't go into a Christian bookshop and buy an off-the-shelf solution. In our globalised, postmodern world people prefer the choice of the pick 'n' mix counter to the 'one size fits all' understanding of the world.

● Your church may be very happy with your current involvement in global mission and see no need for developing a strategy.

● The thought of developing a strategy for global mission might seem like cloud cuckoo land if your church currently has no involvement and no interest.

● You might be perfectly happy with continuing to support your denominational or other mission agency and see no need to get any more involved.

Developing a full-blown programme of direct involvement in global mission for your church is in a sense, one end of the spectrum of possibilities. In light of the changes happening in the world and God's call to us to get involved, we believe that some form of involvement is not an optional extra for those so inclined. Wherever you and your church is now, there are inevitably steps that you can take to become more effective.

Think 'transition'

Many churches have committed themselves over a number of years to supporting particular people working in other parts of the world, or specific projects or organisations. Whilst all of these would probably rejoice to hear that their supporting church wants to get far more actively engaged in global mission, the consequences of a sudden withdrawal of support could be dire. The key issue here is to think in terms of transition. You may now be clear about where you want your church to get to in terms of its involvement in global mission, but it is likely that it will take some time to make the journey from here to there. Unceremoniously pulling the plug on existing commitments is probably not the right strategy!

It is advisable to take a long-term view to phasing out commitments that no longer fit with your global mission strategy. The most sensitivity and time is required in the support of people sent out. One approach would be to guarantee an existing level of support to particular people for as long as they stay working in mission. Another would be to continue support for the remainder of a person's current contract but give notification that it will not be renewed after that.

Summary

❑ There are lots of different ways for a church to get involved in global mission. It is important therefore that you think strategically about the most appropriate ways forward for your church.

❑ The key is to understand who you are and what the global interests are within your congregation and build on these – rather than take on some mission agenda detached from your reality.

Questions for discussion

1. Can you identify good things about the way your church currently approaches global mission, and things you would like to change?

2. Would it help if the church drew up a focused, deliberate, strategy?

3. What new approaches to mission would increase your own interest and desire to be involved in global mission (see Chapter 8 for some ideas)?

Further resources on strategy

Bryan Knell, *Encouraging World Mission*, Administry How-to Guide, vol. 2, no. 9 (2000).

Think Global, Act Local – A Series of Information Papers on How to Involve Your Church with the Wider World produced by Global Connections.

Both these can be obtained from:

Global Connections
Whitefield House
186 Kennington Park Road
London SE11 4BT
Tel: 020 7207 2156
Website: www.globalconnections.co.uk
Email: info@globalconnections.co.uk

10

Doing it Well

As the local church becomes a key player in global mission exciting possibilities open up, but there is a responsibility on the church to ensure that they do it well. It is worth therefore taking a look at some of the issues that can arise so that they can be navigated around rather than being the rocks on which shipwrecks occur!

L-plates please!

When western Christians have contact with Christians in countries of the southern hemisphere they are often bowled over by qualities such as hospitality, spiritual passion and whole-life commitment. It is easy to dream of helping them to achieve a better material quality of life while having our own faith revitalised, and to see the whole project surrounded by a rosy romantic glow. While such a dream can indeed be realised (as many of the churches mentioned in this book have proved), it may often only be after a process of trial and error and considerable heartache.

Direct contact by well-meaning westerners with people who live near the breadline will not always have beneficial outcomes, especially if the westerners are naïve, free with their money and think they know best. The problems we encounter in our own churches and denominations can raise their heads in churches anywhere, and stories of fraud, corruption, self-interest, denominational rivalries, and sexual temptation can be found in churches across the world. So we need to enter into building cross-cultural relationships with the wisdom of serpents as well as the innocence of doves. Just as when we first get behind the wheel of a car we accept L-plates to show others and ourselves that we are new at this, so we need to enter into this new era in global mission with the attitude of learners.

One factor which rears its head time and again is the issue of money.

Money, money, money

Access to western funds can pose huge temptations to people living in poverty, however upright and honest they may be. In many cultures, the availability or even appearance of outside money may raise intense family or community pressures to share the goodies. Such cultural differences and expectations can often create damaging misunderstandings where attitudes to money, accountability and ownership are radically different.

Members of one church that started building a relationship in East Africa discovered that if an African told a westerner about a need and the westerner expressed sympathy, the African believed that the westerner had agreed to provide the money to meet the need. Of course, the westerners had no such intentions and the ensuing misunderstandings were distressing for both sides.

When western Christians decide to 'solve' the problems of poverty in a poor Christian community in the Two-Thirds World by giving generously, here are just some of the problems that can arise:

● The relationship can become unequal.

● The poorer partner can become unhealthily dependent.

● Control over money puts power into the hands of the richer partner who tells the poorer partner what to do.

● It can corrupt the Christians on the receiving end – however honest and upright a person may be, putting massive temptation in their way can corrupt even the most well-meaning leaders.

● If pastors are provided by the western partner with what are, by local standards, large salaries or expensive cars, it can make them feel answerable more to their western paymasters than to their congregations. It may also cause envy among fellow pastors in their area.

● Local ownership of a church, mission or project is essential to its survival and development. The input of funds from outside can result in a loss of local owner-ship so that its local credibility is affected and the local Christians may become passive, failing to take respon-sibility either financially or in other ways.

● Western support for projects, e.g. schools or clinics, in one village can cause jealousy in neighbouring villages or churches.

● Members of the poorer congregation become dissatis-fied with their lot and expect the richer partner to go on providing for them. They may even expect to be found a way to move out of their relatively poor community and into their partners' where they can enjoy a better standard of living.

> The pastor of one church in East Africa felt hurt that the full costs of his retirement home had not been paid for by the community's British friends. His successor asked for an expenses-paid trip to the UK.

In view of these dangers, one might conclude that it is better not to give any money at all – it certainly would avoid a lot of difficulties. But in a world of massive economic inequality it is impossible to take finance out of the equation. When writing to the church in Corinth, Paul talks about giving between churches as 'a matter of equality ... At the present time your plenty will supply what they need' (2 Cor. 8:13-15). The epistle of James chapter 2, verses 14-17 suggests that a Christian who sees a brother or sister in need, blesses them, but does nothing about their physical needs, is not showing a living faith. Believers in Tanzania, or Chad, or India are our brothers and sisters in Christ, so how can we see their need at close quarters and yet turn away? The extremes of poverty and wealth in our world are testament to human selfishness and greed. The global church needs to begin to demonstrate to the rest of humanity what equality is all about and find ways of making our world a fairer place.

> 'Dependency is more closely aligned with biblical teaching than independence. No one is alone in the church ... How can we carry one another's burden without being dependent?'[1]

---

[1] Alex Araujo, *Freedom and Dependency in Christian Partnerships* (Unpublished MS, 1996).

While the dangers described are very real, it is possible to minimise them. There is a lot we can learn from agencies and churches that have been transferring money to Christian ministries in poorer countries for years. Here are some guidelines:

1. Ideally a local church should be self-supporting financially and in other ways, except when starting up. In most circumstances it is therefore not a good idea to commit to paying ongoing costs for a church. However in parts of Africa, for example, pastors often have to support themselves and their families as well as carry out pastoral duties because the community is genuinely too poor to support them. In such circumstances, well-judged financial assistance to pastors may be of vital benefit in relieving stress and enabling them to devote more time to pastoral work.

> *Bournemouth Family Church* raised £2,800 which was divided amongst 52 very poor pastors in Uganda to enable them to set up home-based projects in order to provide support for themselves, their families, churches and communities. The resulting projects included a brickworks, various fruit plantations, and animal husbandry involving pigs, cows or goats. BFC monitored the results and were delighted to see the real benefits which these projects were giving the pastors' families, providing hope for the future and raising their self-esteem.

2. Contributions from outside to a special church project, such as a church building or a community facility, are less likely to be problematic than ongoing funding of core activities, as they have a specific goal and an end-time.

3. Cultural differences with regard to transferring, handling, and accounting for money should be identified early and discussed frankly with a partner before any money is transferred.

4. The issue of unhealthy dependency and how to avoid it should also be discussed openly between the partners before any money is given.

5. At both ends guidance should be agreed from the start on how any requests for money from individuals or groups, made to individual church members or the church, should be handled (see below on how St Mary's and St Paul's, Thornbury, approached this issue).

'If I say that I will supply the material for you to build a church building but only if it is built the way I want it, I am exercising undue control. But if I learn that you have a plan to build a church building and offer to help provide the materials for you to build it as you see fit, no unhealthy control is involved. It is only undue control when I insist that you do things my way in order to get my help. If the giver can give without the need for control and if the receiver can receive without being stifled, financial dependency ceases to be a problem.'[2]

---

6. It helps to set agreed, measurable objectives (such as completion of a church building).

7. Agreed ground rules and suitable accountability arrangements should be put in place to ensure so far as possible that money is used for the intended purposes.

8. It is better all round to deal with a team in the partnering church, rather than a single person.

---

[2] Araujo, *Freedom and Dependency*, pp.312-13.

9. Despite best efforts there will remain an element of risk when there is accountability without control. This is where a refusal to rush into transferring funds until real confidence has been built can pay dividends.

10. Using money in a way that empowers those receiving it and gives them dignity is to be preferred wherever possible. For example, giving money to individuals, groups or churches to set up their own businesses and so generate ongoing income may literally be a lifeline. But it might be even better for their self-respect to *lend* the money on a favourable basis, to be repaid out of income generated. That way, you would have an ongoing fund to help still more people.

In 2002 *St John's, Blackheath*, set up an agricultural cooperative of ten farmers in a village in Tanzania. Each farmer was lent £500 and given training on the understanding (set out in written agreements) that they would repay the loan within five to ten years so that more people could be helped in a similar way.

Take advice!

We've been emphasising the exciting possibilities available for ordinary Christians to get involved in mission in the joined-up world we now live in, but also warning of the risks. If you want to start a cross-cultural partnership or go yourself to do mission in another country, it would be utter folly not to take advice from those who know about the subject. We're talking of course about mission and development agencies. They are the experts in mission and in the practicalities of sending, funding and giving all round support to those going to do mission work.

HEALTH HAZARDS

AIDS is prevalent in most of Sub-Saharan Africa and a growing threat in many other countries of the world. It is vital to ensure that suitable precautions are taken on this and other health issues before visiting many countries outside the West. Interhealth, a Christian agency specialising in health advice and treatment for those who travel worldwide, is well-placed to advise on these issues and can provide tailor-made advice and medical packs. Contact: Interhealth, 157 Waterloo Road, London SE1 8US. Tel: 020 7902 9000. Fax: 020 7928 0927. Email: info@interhealth.org.uk

Some of these organisations still believe that it's best for you not to get involved at all but simply to support them. Most however have woken up to the realities of this global era and are keen to work with individuals, churches and other groups to make the most of the interest and resources that can be released. Whether you want information about a particular place, help in how to support people living overseas, or assistance in setting up a visit, there are organisations that can help.

Altrincham Baptist Church embarked on its partnership with Christians in Jinja, Uganda, because they believed God told them to. But they recognised their own ignorance and took advice about Uganda from the African Pastors' Fellowship and from members of their congregation with firsthand experience of doing mission there.

There are also books available that give practical advice on many aspects of doing mission abroad. Some of them are listed at the end of this chapter.

The story of *St Mary's and St Paul's, Thornbury*, and their link with Bufumbo, Uganda, offers useful guidelines on some of the issues raised in this chapter.

Because of the close involvement of a CMS regional representative in the initial stages of the Thornbury-Bufumbo link (see under 'Take your Partners' in Chapter 8), cultural and other difficulties were generally anticipated and managed. A crucial factor in getting the relationship going was the fact that the link at the Bufumbo end was headed initially by an individual, and then by a small group, whom the Thornbury churches felt able to trust.

St Mary's and St Paul's were giving money towards the establishment of a much needed health centre in Bufumbo, and put the following arrangements in place:

● The Ugandans make proposals for projects to be funded by Thornbury, which may accept or decline to get involved. But Thornbury does not tell the Ugandans what they need, nor impose their own ideas on exactly how money given for a project should be spent.

● No money is given from UK individuals to Ugandan individuals. Everything goes from St Mary's/St Paul's to the Ugandan church. Whenever a Ugandan makes a request they are asked to route it via the church to ensure the church approves it.

▶

- Money is drip fed from the UK in irregular amounts (of no more than £1,000), rather than one really big lump. This means the temptation to mis-appropriate it is less overwhelming.

- When any money is sent, the St Mary's accountant writes to inform *all* the members of the Ugandan church team responsible for managing the funds so that they all know when money is coming, and how much.

- St Mary's/St Paul's regularly receive copies of receipts and bank statements. They are sometimes also sent estimates, and have occasionally queried them or suggested seeking another quote.

- They recognise that once the money has gone into the church account they cannot track it further. But they receive regular photos as well as written reports on how the project is progressing, will see the results for themselves once it is completed, and are pretty confident that finances are being handled properly.

St Mary's and St Paul's wanted to bring some members of the Bufumbo congregation to Thornbury. Bringing visitors from an overseas partner church to the UK should not be undertaken lightly. The visitors could be overwhelmed by culture shock, or so bedaz-zled by the apparent affluence of life in the UK that they conclude their UK friends should be giving them far more money than they had so far seen! Here again St Mary's/St Paul's were able to draw on CMS's long experience, and with their advice carefully prepared people at both ends for the cultural and economic dif-ferences. As a result the inward visit in 2001 was a huge success for both sides.

Ready, aim, fire!

Some management gurus exhort their disciples to 'Fire, aim, ready' in today's fast-paced world. Things are moving so quickly, they say, that you simply don't have time to prepare before you pull the trigger on your next product, reorganisation or merger. Well things are moving quickly and speed of response is becoming increasingly important but it would be a great mistake for us all to swallow this particular recipe.

The global era is opening up huge new opportunities for those brave enough to take them. God calls his people to get involved in the world and to be salt and light in every corner. Our mandate is to get stuck in – to use the tools at our disposal to the best possible effect in the global mission to which we are called. Fire! is what guns are made to do – not to be polished and greased, or simply adorn a wall. As God's people, we are called to action but we must first go through the process of 'ready' and 'aim'. Alongside the new opportunities are new pitfalls. Jumping in without thought and understanding will lead to casualties. Seeing the threats and staying in our comfort zones is not an option. We all need to put on the L-plates, learn what we can and tread boldly into an exciting future.

Summary

❑ There are certain areas in which it is common for difficulties to arise when doing mission direct. It helps if you go into it with a learning attitude.

❑ Beware of romanticising Christians from another part of the global church. They are human too, and contact with westerners can create special temptations and stresses for them.

▶

▶

□ Money is an issue! It can be a great blessing to share God-given resources and it can be the nail in the coffin of a relationship.

□ Most of these pitfalls can be avoided or minimised through careful forethought – so think!

□ Seek advice from agencies or others who understand the other culture and church scene.

Questions for discussion

1. Do you think money should form any part of a church-to-church relationship?

2. Do you think the likely benefits of setting up a partnership between your church and one in a poorer area of the world outweigh the potential risks?

Further resources on doing it well

Global Connections Code of Best Practice in Short-Term Mission outlines the issues anyone setting up any kind of limited-term mission involvement needs to address. Available from Global Connections, Whitefield House, 186 Kennington Park Road, London SE11 4BT. Tel: 020 7 207 2156. Email: info@globalconnections.co.uk.

Ross Paterson, *Explaining Mission* (Tunbridge: Sovereign World, 1993) – a useful and readable book that is full of challenge.

Michael Griffiths, *Lambs Dancing with Wolves – a Manual for Christian Workers Overseas* (Grand Rapids, MI: Kregel

Publications, 2001) – includes a lot of practical information for new missionaries.

Margaret Wardell and Robin Thomson, *Entering Another's World*, St John's Extension Studies – valuable material for those preparing to work in another's culture.

Ditch Townsend, *Stop, Check, Go – A Practical Guide for Cross-Cultural Teamwork* (Carlisle: OM Publishing, 1996) – written for people planning to go on short-term (i.e. several weeks or months) team trips, it contains practical information and advice.

Ian and Jean Gateley, *My Reasonable Service? Practical Suggestions for the Christian Working Overseas* (Durham: Pentland Press, 1996).

Richard Briggs (ed.), *Global Action – A Personal Discipleship Manual for the World Christian* (Carlisle: OM Publishing, 1997) – an excellent study manual to prepare for mission work in other cultures; suitable for individuals or groups.

Ted Lankaster, *The Travellers' Good Health Guide* (London: Sheldon Press, 1999) – a guide to staying healthy abroad.

Peter Jordan, *Re-entry: Making the Transition from Missions to Life at Home* (YWAM, 1992).

Returning from Short-Term Mission, a short booklet produced by Global Connections (contact details above) on the readjustment process.

A final word

We hope that this book has stimulated you. You may react against some of the things we are suggesting but we hope that you have been challenged to think about what the future of global mission might look like.

In writing about the future and trying to point out the way ahead we inevitably open ourselves up to embarrassment as that future unfolds. As people deeply committed to global mission, our intention is to inspire a whole new movement of God's people to take seriously their privilege and responsibility to the global church and take the Good News into every corner of the world. This may be the end of one book but we passionately believe that it is only the very beginning of something new. We pray that Connect! will become a movement – an unstoppable avalanche. If this book in some small way helps to get that avalanche started then it will have done its job.

Watch for more Connect! resources that are planned: more books, events, videos and practical tools to get you up and running. Keep an eye on www.connect.nu for the latest information and send us your thoughts and experience.

Equipping Christians to live actively, biblically and wholeheartedly for Christ — that's the goal of all that Spring Harvest does.

The Main Event

The largest Christian event of its kind in Europe — an Easter-time gathering of over 60,000 people for learning, worship and fun. The programme includes varied and inspiring choices for everyone, no matter how old or young, and no matter where you are in your Christian life.

Resources

- *Books* to help you understand issues that matter — prayer, family issues, Bible themes, workplace and more
- *Music albums* introducing new songs and showcasing live worship from the Main Event each year
- *Childrens resources* including popular music albums and songbooks
- *Songbooks* to introduce the best new worship material each year
- *Audio tapes* of teaching from Spring Harvest — a selection of thousands is available to choose from
- *Youth pastoral resources, songwords projection software, video services and more...*

Conferences

- *Youthwork the conference* — for volunteer youth workers, run in partnership with Youthwork magazine, YFC, Oasis Youth Action and the Salvation Army

- *At Work Together* to equip workers to effectively live and witness for Christ in today's challenging workplace.

Le Pas Opton is a beautiful four star holiday site on the French Vendée coast, exclusively owned and operated by Spring Harvest. Mobile homes, tents or your own tent/tourer — take your choice at this delightful resort where you'll find top quality facilities and excellent service.

Our aim at *Le Pas Opton* is to give you the opportunity for relaxation and refreshment of body, mind and spirit. Call Spring Harvest Holidays on 0870 060 3322 for a free brochure.

INVESTOR IN PEOPLE

For more information contact our Customer Service team on 01825 769000 or visit our website at www.springharvest.org

Spring Harvest. A Registered Charity.